THE PRICE THEORY OF VALUE IN PUBLIC FINANCE

by Donald R. Escarraz

UNIVERSITY OF FLORIDA PRESS / GAINESVILLE, FLORIDA, 1966

LIBRARY OF CONGRESS
CATALOG CARD NO. 66-64915

PRINTED BY THE PARAMOUNT PRESS
JACKSONVILLE, FLORIDA

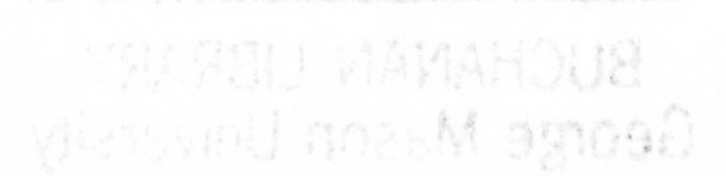

CONTENTS

UNIVERSITY OF FLORIDA MONOGRAPHS

Social Sciences

1. *The Whigs of Florida, 1845-1854,* by H. J. Doherty, Jr.

2. *Austrian Catholics and the Social Question, 1918-1933,* by A. Diamant.

3. *The Siege of St. Augustine in 1702,* by C. W. Arnade

4. *New Light on Early and Medieval Japanese Historiography,* by J. A. Harrison

5. *The Swiss Press and Foreign Affairs in World War II,* by F. H. Hartmann

6. *The American Militia: Decade of Decision, 1789-1800,* by J. K. Mahon

7. *The Foundation of Jacques Maritain's Political Philosophy,* by H. Y. Jung

8. *Latin American Population Studies,* by T. L. Smith

9. *Jacksonian Democracy on the Florida Frontier,* by A. W. Thompson

10. *Holman Versus Hughes: Extension of Australian Commonwealth Powers,* by C. Joyner

11. *Welfare Economics and Subsidy Programs,* by M. Z. Kafoglis

12. *Tribune of the Slavophiles: Konstantin Aksakov,* by E. Chmielewski

13. *City Managers in Politics: An Analysis of Manager Tenure and Termination,* by G. M. Kammerer, C. D. Farris, J. M. DeGrove, and A. B. Clubok

14. *Recent Southern Economic Development as Revealed by the Changing Structure of Employment,* by E. S. Dunn, Jr.

15. *Sea Power and Chilean Independence,* by D. E. Worcester

16. *The Sherman Antitrust Act and Foreign Trade,* by A. Simmons

17. *The Origins of Hamilton's Fiscal Policies,* by D. F. Swanson

18. *Criminal Asylum in Anglo-Saxon Law,* by C. H. Riggs, Jr.

19. *Colonia Barón Hirsch, A Jewish Agricultural Colony in Argentina,* by M. D. Winsberg

20. *Time Deposits in Present-day Commercial Banking,* by L. L. Crum

21. *The Eastern Greenland Case in Historical Perspective,* by O. Svarlien

22. *Jacksonian Democracy and the Historians,* by A. A. Cave

23. *The Rise of the American Chemistry Profession, 1850-1900,* by E. H. Beardsley

24. *Aymara Communities and the Bolivian Agrarian Reform,* by W. E. Carter

25. *Conservatives in the Progressive Era: The Taft Republicans of 1912,* by N. M. Wilensky

26. *The Anglo-Norwegian Fisheries Case of 1951 and the Changing Law of the Territorial Sea,* by T. Kobayashi

27. *The Liquidity Structure of Firms and Monetary Economics,* by W. J. Frazer, Jr.

28. *Russo-Persian Commercial Relations, 1828-1914,* by M. L. Entner

29. *The Imperial Policy of Sir Robert Borden,* by H. A. Wilson

30. *The Association of Income and Educational Achievement,* by R. L. Lassiter, Jr.

31. *The Relation of the People to the Land in Southern Iraq,* by F. Baali

32. *The Price Theory of Value in Public Finance,* by D. R. Escarraz

PREFACE

The voluntary exchange or price theory of public finance has a history which is as long as the history of the price theory of private goods, if the number of years is the basis for the length of history. However, very few economists have attempted to develop the theory further as an explanation of political or economic behavior or to apply it as a criterion for policy decisions of government. The theory has not reached the degree of acceptability which the price theory of private goods has reached.

This difference in acceptability can be explained in part by the existence of certain criticisms of the price theory of public finance which are not relevant to, or at least have never been raised with respect to, the price theory of private goods. Another part of the difference may be explained by the absence of the development of a general framework in the price theory of public finance which could be used for a wide range of problems and which could be used to indicate the relationship of the two theories.

This monograph attempts to approach both of the above factors which have to some extent limited the acceptability of the price theory of public finance among economists. The final chapter illustrates some of the uses of the theory in the past and the prospects of its acceptance by more economists in the future.

There is no doubt that the critique of criticisms of the theory presented here is incomplete. Indeed, there may exist errors in interpretation and analysis both with respect to the critique of criticisms and with respect to the suggested approach. However, if more issues are clarified by the presentation than are confused, the author will consider that he has achieved the purpose of the monograph. The field is currently confused, and yet it is one which may have a tremendous potential. Therefore, the monograph may have value even if it does not clarify issues but does cause other economists to reconsider the field, and they as a result clarify the issues.

My indebtedness is acknowledged to Dr. Ansel M. Sharp who started me into the study of the price theory of public finance and led me through a dissertation on the subject at Oklahoma State University. I am also indebted to Dr. Milton Z. Kafoglis of the University of Florida for his encouragement. It was Dr. Kafoglis who originally suggested that my dissertation should be published and then urged me on to incorporate in it my latest work in the field. The result is that less than half of the original dissertation is contained in this monograph.

I also wish to express my thanks to the editors and readers for the Social Sciences Monograph Series for their comments and suggestions, and to the typing pool of the College of Business Administration for their prompt and efficient service. Finally, but not least, I wish to thank my wife and three children for putting up with me during the many months of writing, rewriting, and waiting that have gone into this monograph. The author of any original work goes through much but his family undoubtedly suffer more.

DONALD RAY ESCARRAZ

1. INTRODUCTION

The voluntary exchange or price theory of public finance had its origin in the benefit approach to taxation, but it never has had the widespread acceptance enjoyed by that approach in the eighteenth and nineteenth centuries. The causes of this lack of acceptance are the primary theme of this monograph. More specifically, an attempt is made to show that the criticisms of the theory are not a sufficient reason to completely reject it. In the process of analyzing the major criticisms, suggested approaches to the theory and applications to the political process are presented.

There are many aspects to the voluntary exchange approach to public finance, but its essence can be understood by simply considering it to be the application of the whole body of price theory to the problem of the supply of goods and services by the government. This view of public finance requires that the revenues of the government (taxes) be considered together with the expenditures of the government. The expenditures must be considered as costs of producing public goods and services. The government is, thus, a producer or firm in the economy, similar to private firms. Economists have not generally accepted this concept. In fact, economists have often discussed the expenditure activities of the government in terms of its being a consumer. The notion of the government as a consumer may have been an outgrowth of Adam Smith's belief that some of the expenditures of the sovereign are for unproductive labor. The unproductive-labor concept has dropped out of economic literature, but not the concept that the government consumes goods and services when it makes expenditures. The non-acceptance of the concept of the government as a producer enters the discussion throughout this monograph.

The most important theoretical concepts which must be accepted with the price theory of public finance are related to the revealing of preferences for public goods. The theory implies that public goods do provide satisfaction to the individual and that the individual associates the satisfaction with the quantity of the public goods available to him. It also implies that the individual will reveal his preferences for public goods if given the opportunity. The non-acceptance of these concepts is discussed in the first part of Chapter 3.

Richard A. Musgrave has placed importance on the determination of a single best solution in the allocation of resources when public goods are involved. This determination is treated in the last part of Chapter 3 and in Chapter 4. The latter chapter also suggests an approach to the price theory of public finance. A model is developed which attempts to show a single best solution analogous to the Pareto optimum.

The price theory of public finance does require that taxes be viewed as a price paid for goods and services. The taxpayer is a taxpayer-buyer. If the political organization is taken into consideration, the taxpayer can be considered a voter-buyer, since he indicates the quantity of goods and services he desires through his vote rather than through the taxes paid. Taxes are the prices paid for the goods and services actually supplied, but the determination of what quantities of goods and services should be supplied is based on the taxpayers' voting in the political process. Therefore, the determination of the individual's taxes constitutes the allocation of the value or costs of the goods and services. Economists have not generally accepted this concept of taxes as a price or as an allocation of value or costs. In fact, taxes are often considered to be little more than a form of coercive activity of government which is inherent in the nature of the state. These problems are discussed in Chapter 5.

That the taxpayer is a voter-buyer may thus be implied by the price theory of public finance. In any case, the concept of the voter-buyer does imply the existence of a particular type of political mechanism. The voter-buyer not only must want to reveal his preferences for public goods, he must have a means by which to do so. Therefore, the political mechanism cannot be ignored by an economist accepting the price theory of public finance. The effect of the political mechanism upon the degree of coercion in taxation is discussed in the last part of Chapter 5.

The suggested approach of Chapter 4 and the approach adopted to analyze the criticisms in Chapter 5 become the basis for possible applications of the price theory of public finance in Chapter 6. Chapter 7 backs up to take a look at some existing applications of the theory by economists and to look at the prospects for further applications by other economists.

Richard A. Musgrave and Alan T. Peacock, *Classics in the Theory of Public Finance*, is a minimum requirement to place the arguments presented here in proper historical perspective. Musgrave, *The Theory of Public Finance*, is necessary background for the specific criticisms that are discussed here, and for seeing the basis upon which the suggested approach was developed. An attempt has been made to present Musgrave's criticisms and his adaptation of Paul A. Samuelson's model, but these are not a substitute for reading Musgrave's original work, since his criticisms are lifted out of the context in which they were presented.

2. GRAPHICAL MODELS

The development of the voluntary exchange theory of public finance since the turn of the century has centered around three graphical models and Knut Wicksell's concept of unanimity. To be sure, other writings since the turn of the century are directly or indirectly related to the voluntary exchange or price theory in public finance, but the graphical models with Wicksell's unanimity principle sufficiently bring out the main points of the approach. Therefore in this chapter there is an attempt made to restate three of the geometric models and to state the unanimity principle in graphical form, so that the main points of the theory can be understood and the interrelationships among the presentations can be recognized. Musgrave's criticisms of the Lindahl model are also considered in this chapter because they have been a stumbling block to the general understanding and acceptance of the approach in the United States.

Erik Lindahl and Knut Wicksell

In 1919 Erik Lindahl, a Swedish economist,[1] presented a simple graphical model which attempted to establish the total expenditure on a public good and the relative tax shares of two classes of society. Class A (the relatively well-to-do) are represented by legislators A and class B (the relatively poor) are represented by legislators B. It is assumed that there is an even distribution of political power between the two groups. It is also assumed that all economically related public services are lumped together so that the total cost is the total cost of a group of services rather than a single service.

Figure 1 shows on the abscissa the relative share of the total cost of providing a given public good. Reading from left to right is the relative share of A, and reading from right to left is the relative share of B. Various levels of total cost (V through Z) are shown along the ordinate. The curve AR indicates the total expenditure on the public service at various relative cost shares to which legislators A would agree. Logically, A legislators are willing to have a greater total expenditure made, if class A of society can pay a smaller percentage of the total

1. See Musgrave and Peacock, pp. 168-76, for a translated chapter from Lindahl, *Die Gerechtigkeit der Besteuerung*. (Full information on cited works is in the Bibliography.)

cost. The curve BS indicates the total expenditure on the public service at various relative cost shares to which legislators B would agree. At X level of total expenditure, group A would agree only if group B would pay 60 per cent of the total cost, while group B would agree only if group A would pay 72 per cent of the total cost.

The equilibrium solution is clearly at the intersection of the two curves at P. The total expenditure to be made on the group of public services is Y. A agrees to pay 60 per cent of Y, while B agrees to pay 40 per cent of Y.

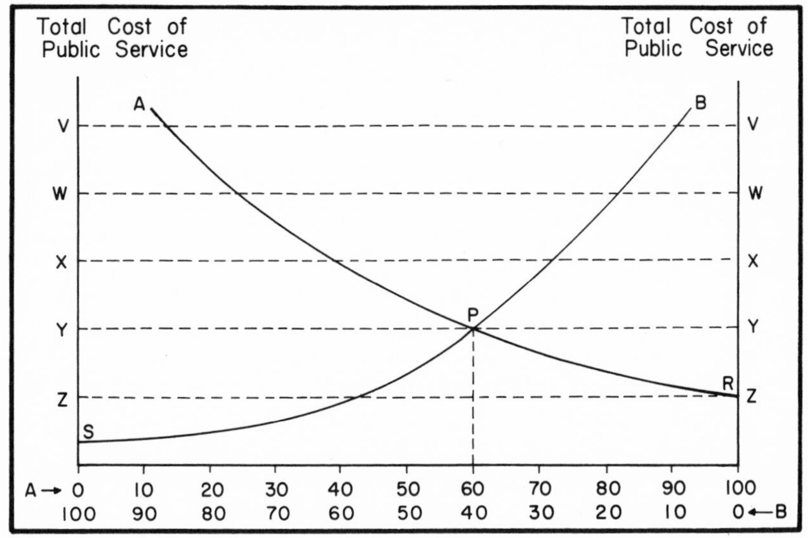

Figure 1.

The fact that the Lindahl model emphasizes the political process in the determination of how much should be supplied and who should pay for the service in a manner consistent with the political principles laid down by Knut Wicksell has been recognized.[2] However, a presentation of the Lindahl model in terms of Wicksell's unanimity principle[3] may be useful before evaluating the criticisms of the Lindahl model.

In Figure 2 the Lindahl model is traced by the dashed curves AR

2. Musgrave, "Voluntary Exchange Theory of Public Finance," p. 215; Musgrave, *Theory of Public Finance*, p. 74.

3. See Musgrave and Peacock, pp. 72-118, for a translation of Wicksell's statement of the principle; see Uhr, *Economic Doctrines of Knut Wicksell*, pp. 164-80, and B. Seligman, *Main Currents in Modern Economics*, pp. 559-60, for interpretations.

and BS, with main bill A representing a total expenditure of V, amendment A′, a total expenditure of W, etc. Reading the graph in terms of Wicksell's unanimity principle, the abscissa reading right to left measures the percentage of group B who would vote for various expenditure bills with various tax plans. Tax plan a favors group B while tax

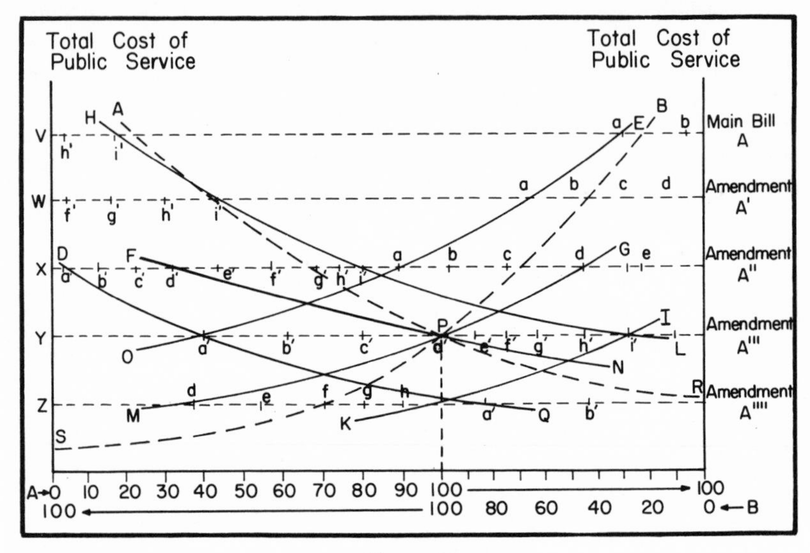

Figure 2.

plan i favors group A. These tax plans can be converted into the terminology of the Lindahl model with the following schedule.

Tax Plan	A	B
a	90% of total cost	10% of total cost
b	80% " " "	20% " " "
c	70% " " "	30% " " "
d	60% " " "	40% " " "
e	50% " " "	50% " " "
f	40% " " "	60% " " "
g	30% " " "	70% " " "
h	20% " " "	80% " " "
i	10% " " "	90% " " "

The curve DQ connecting all of the a′ points indicates the percentage of A legislators who would vote for the various expenditure proposals with tax plan a (i.e., class A of society to pay 90 per cent of the total cost). The curve EO connecting all of the a points indicates the percentage of B legislators who would vote for the various expenditure proposals with tax plan a (i.e., class B of society to pay 10 per cent of the total cost). The only proposal which can obtain perfect unanimity is Amendment A‴ with tax plan d. In terms of the Lindahl model it is the Y level of total cost with class A paying 60 per cent of Y and class B paying 40 per cent of Y. On Amendment A″ with tax plan g, none of the B legislators and only 65 per cent of the A legislators would vote for the proposal. On Amendment A″ with tax plan c only 15 per cent of the A legislators and 75 per cent of the B legislators would vote for the proposal.[4]

Both Wicksell and Lindahl, however, recognized the practical limitation that the legislature probably would never be restricted by a perfect unanimity rule. Therefore, Wicksell accepted the concept of approximate unanimity, and Lindahl discussed the effects of dropping the assumption of equal political power. The result of either of these practical considerations may be that equilibrium can be achieved in an area around point P, depending upon which bill and tax plan approximating Amendment A‴ with tax plan d is voted on first or which group in society has an advantage in political power.

More specifically using just the Wicksell model, the equilibrium level of expenditure and tax plan can be seen to depend upon the level of unanimity required and the order in which the proposals are voted upon. Assuming 100 legislators in group A and 100 in group B, and assuming that the majority rule is accepted as approximate unanimity, equilibrium can take place for Amendment A⁗ with any tax plan, because all of the tax plans will get 100 per cent of the vote of the B legislators and enough of the vote of the A legislators to make a majority vote. Tax plan a or b would also be accepted as an equilibrium proposal with Amendment A″. With Amendment A‴ any of the tax plans, b, c, d, e, f, or g, will be accepted under the majority rule concept of approximate unanimity. The exact combination of bill and tax plan to be accepted would depend entirely on which one was first presented for a vote.[5]

According to Lindahl, if unequal political power exists, the solution will lie on SPR of the Lindahl model in Figure 1. BPS is the total

4. With the Wicksell-Lindahl model, the question of what goods should be supplied by the government is also determined because only those goods which are capable of receiving perfect unanimity should be supplied.

5. Wicksell suggests that, in the case of approximate unanimity, all proposals should be voted on and the one with the greatest total vote be accepted. This requirement would limit the equilibrium solutions to Amendment A‴ with tax plan d and Amendment A⁗ with any of the tax plans, since these are the proposals which would receive a 100 per cent yes vote of one group or the other.

expenditure which the B legislators would desire at varying tax sharing plans and APR is the total expenditure which the A legislators would desire at varying tax sharing plans. PS is the segment of BPS which is capable of obtaining perfect unanimity and PR is the segment of APR which is capable of obtaining perfect unanimity. Therefore, with Lindahl's concept of unequal political power, which is in terms of one group's ability to force its desires upon the other group, the solution will lie on PS if B has the greater political power and on PR if A has the greater political power. However, if unequal political power is accepted as being any solution reached by compromise other than the optimum solution which can be reached with perfect unanimity, the equilibrium can be a large number of solutions around the point P in Figure 2. No matter what political conditions exist or which concept of political power is accepted, the combined Wicksell-Lindahl model would appear to be useful in explaining the results of the political process. Equilibrium will take place around point P in any case, and all that would remain is to accurately evaluate the political process in order to determine the actual equilibrium which will take place.

In February, 1939, Musgrave published an article with an interpretation of Lindahl's model, but Musgrave's conclusions were the opposite of those arrived at in the foregoing interpretation of the Wicksell-Lindahl model. "To summarize: as an interpretation of the actual expenditure process, the voluntary exchange theory was found unacceptable because of the unrealistic nature of the voluntary exchange assumption in general and of the competitive pricing assumption in particular. As a solution to the theory of tax justice it was found strictly dependent upon the premise of competitive pricing; the definition of the justice problem employed, moreover, appeared excessively narrow. As standards of reference for analysis and appraisal of actual revenue-expenditure policies, the voluntary exchange model and its corollary, the neutral revenue-expenditure process, were found unacceptable."[6]

Musgrave's rejection of the theory in general because of the unrealistic nature of the voluntary exchange assumption is based on the fact that "direct compulsion prevails in the legal enforcement of individual tax contributions, independently of the individual's willingness to share a part of the burden."[7] However, one answer to this criticism is that the

6. "Voluntary Exchange Theory," p. 231. The voluntary exchange theory as a standard of reference for analysis and for the meaning and importance of the neutral revenue-expenditure process is the primary concern of the monograph; see especially Chapters 5 and 6.

7. Taxes as a form of coercion will be considered in more detail in Chapter 5.

situation in the private economy cannot be said to be very different. In the private economy, an individual is assumed to have a demand for any particular good which relates the quantities of the good which the individual would want to purchase to various prices. Once the individual has expressed his demand by making the purchase, laws of society, generally, protect the seller from the buyer's changing his mind. In the voluntary exchange model the individual is assumed to have a similar type of demand for each type of public good. The individual, however, permits his representative in the legislature to interpret this demand schedule. Once the legislator has expressed this demand by accepting a particular level of expenditure and tax plan, the purchase has been made. The laws of society, as in the case of the private good, protect the seller from the buyer's changing his mind. Once the demand is expressed by purchase or by the legislators' voting favorably for the providing of a product or service with a particular tax plan, the transaction is completed and laws protect the parties of the sale from changes in the individual's subjective evaluation of the quantity he wants at the price agreed upon.

The problem which Musgrave seems to have discussed under the heading of the compulsive nature of the political process is just the opposite of compulsion.[8] The problem lies in whether or not the fact that compulsion exists affects the individual's expressed demand. In the private economy it is assumed that it does not.[9] In the political process it may be more questionable, but, in the opinion of this writer, Musgrave has not given a sufficient reason for the rejection of the theory in general.

Musgrave's rejection of the theory because of the competitive pricing assumption in particular is just a further statement of his rejection of the theory in general. Musgrave did not recognize the oneness of his two bases for rejection. He did not consider that compulsion exists only after a demand is expressed and that this compulsion is not very dissimilar to the compulsion that exists with a private good once demand has been expressed through a legal purchase of the good. The effects of bargaining power or political power which Musgrave considers are merely an analysis based on an assumption that the exist-

8. It is the opposite of compulsion in that it revolves around the individual's being free to express his demand without compulsion and even to recontract if an equilibrium solution is not determined which is consistent with the demand expressed.

9. There is little or no literature on the economic effects of a private firm giving an absolute guarantee of satisfaction or your money back.

ence of compulsion, after a quantity at a price has been expressed, affects the quantity which would be expressed.

Musgrave's analysis, however, is primarily in terms of the individual's realizing that his expressed demand will affect the price. This analysis is based on Lindahl's statement of the model (i.e., that one individual's demand curve is the other individual's supply curve). Part of the problem, however, seems to be that Musgrave switches his analysis to the individual from the political process.[10] In his analysis the individual recognizes that his expressed demand is going to affect his cost and, therefore, he will not express his true demand.[11] However, if it is remembered that the voluntary exchange model takes place in a political setting, at least part of Musgrave's criticism can be dropped. The individual is not directly bargaining with another individual for the exchange of two goods. Two groups of legislators are attempting to obtain the quantity of a good which the individuals, whom the legislator represents, would want at a price consistent with that quantity. The legislator does not have to obtain the lowest possible price for various quantities to satisfy the individuals he represents. All that the legislator must obtain is a quantity and price relationship which the individuals that he represents consider satisfactory. Therefore, it cannot be assumed that the demand curves will be affected by the fact that the price is affected by the demand expressed by the legislator. Price cannot be removed from its relationship to quantity just because the good under consideration is a public good. If the legislator is attempting to maximize the satisfaction of those individuals whom he represents, he must express a demand which relates quantity and price and it must be a quantity and price relationship indicated by the demand curve in the Lindahl model because this curve by definition is the schedule of quantities which the individuals would want at various prices. To express any other quantity-price relationship would put the legislator in the position of not truly representing the individuals that put him in office. This situation may well exist, but this is not the question. In other

10. This criticism is of particular importance when Musgrave considers the effects of large numbers. If the model is restricted to the political mechanism, the problem of large numbers does not exist in the form stated by Musgrave. The voting on specific expenditure-tax proposals is done by a limited number of legislators representing taxpayer consumers and not by the taxpayer consumers themselves. The problem of the legislator representing a large number of taxpayer consumers is a different problem, and is treated in Chapter 6.

11. The theoretical aspects of the problem of unrevealed preferences are discussed in detail in Chapter 3.

words, Musgrave's criticism although stated in terms of a theoretical criticism is more akin to a practical criticism that politicians do not perfectly represent those who put them in office.[12]

Musgrave in 1959 reconsidered his rejection of the voluntary exchange model and came up with the same conclusions.[13] This time, however, his analysis was more specifically in terms of a Cournot duopoly situation. This analysis can be rejected simply because each individual is not a producer trying to obtain a favorable price for the goods he has to sell. The comments about Musgrave's earlier rejection of the theory still apply, but it may be good to consider further what the Cournot duopoly analysis would imply. An analogy can be made for this purpose. In the private economy, it would have to be assumed that a stockholder of a large company tries to get management to set its price so that the stockholder acting as a consumer can purchase a larger quantity of the good produced by the firm. The stockholder and consumer may be one person, but this does not mean that as a stockholder the individual tries to bargain with other individuals (stockholders) just because by so doing he can affect the price he has to pay for the good as a consumer. In the public economy the individual is a voter and a consumer. This fact, however, does not mean that the individual as a voter will bargain with other voters to affect the price he has to pay for the good as a consumer. The only concern of the individual is that he can purchase a quantity of the good at a price which maximizes his satisfaction. In the case of a private good this is accomplished by merely seeing to it that the quantity he purchases has a particular relationship to the price determined by the market or by the management. In the case of the public good this is accomplished by seeing to it that the legislator who represents the individual expresses a quantity and price relationship that maximizes the individual's satisfaction.

Under the consideration of the voluntary exchange theory as a solution to the theory of tax justice, Musgrave rejects the theory because of the non-competitive nature of the political process and because of the assumption that original distribution of wealth is a "just" distribution. The former cause for rejection has been discussed and only accepted as a practical limitation to the extent that politicians do not and need

12. The theoretical issue involved in the problem is whether or not individuals do consider public goods in terms of a quantity and price relationship which maximizes satisfaction and which they expect their legislators to abide by. This issue is taken up in Chapter 3.

13. *Theory of Public Finance*, pp. 78-80

not abide by the desires of the individuals whom they represent. The latter cause for rejection is much more complex and will not be treated here.[14]

Howard R. Bowen

In 1943 Howard R. Bowen presented another formulation of the voluntary exchange or price theory of public finance, which was in terms of an individual voting process rather than a political voting process, and which was presented more along the lines of accepted price theory analysis.[15]

Figure 3 presents the determination of the ideal output and cost distribution in terms of real goods. The vertical axis measures the quantity of all other goods which the individuals would be willing to give up to obtain social goods, and the horizontal axis measures the quantity of the social good desired. The individual curves of marginal substitution are individual demand curves with prices stated in terms of the quantity of all other goods that the individual is willing to give up to obtain various quantities of social goods.[16] The TMS curve is the total demand curve. Because social goods are defined as those for which the demand (supply)[17] cannot be individually held, the total demand curve is obtained by vertically adding the individual demand curves (MS_a MS_b and MS_c) rather than by horizontally adding them. The intersection of the marginal cost curve (MC)[18] and the total demand curve at point P determines the "ideal" output. The individual cost

14. The nature of the state and the nature of man are important factors in the question of tax justice, but will not be discussed here. For one interpretation of the effect of the nature of the state on the acceptance or non-acceptance of the voluntary exchange theory, see Buchanan, "Pure Theory of Government Finance."

15. "Interpretation of Voting in the Allocation of Economic Resources."

16. Bowen's use of marginal substitution curves instead of regularly defined demand curves is regrettable because it may have contributed to the later use of indifference curves. The adoption of indifference curves by Samuelson and Musgrave has led to considerable confusion and a continued rejection of the theory. The problems developing from Musgrave's analysis are treated at length in Chapter 4.

17. Bowen speaks of divisibility of demand, yet speaks of social goods not being divisible into units that can be the unique possession of individuals. The possession of individuals refers to the consumption of a supply of goods, so that it is actually the indivisibility of supply rather than demand.

18. Bowen uses the concept that the ideal output exists when MC equals demand if the product has constant or decreasing costs but when AC equals demand if the product has increasing costs. Bowen explains the methodology in the latter case as well as the first two cases, but no attempt is made to present the AC determination since MC determination is still the more widely held concept.

shares are determined by the intersection of the vertical line at the "ideal" output and the individual demand curves.[19]

Bowen also shows that the average total demand (TMS/N) and average marginal cost (MC/N) would determine the same "ideal" output (P). The slope of the TMS curve and the TMS/N curve would not be

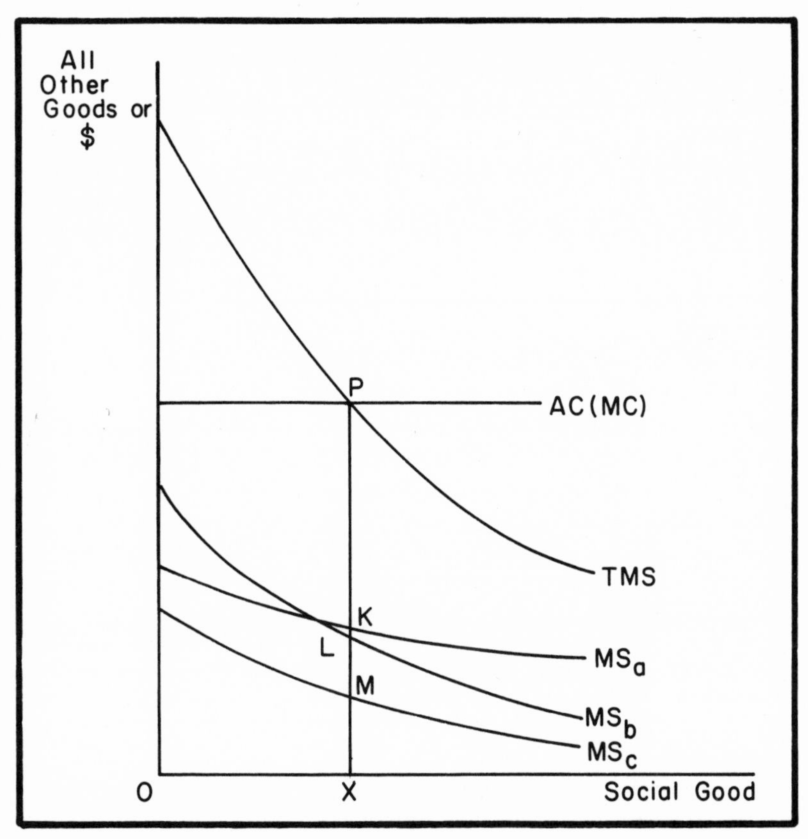

Figure 3.

the same, but the point of intersection would be the same because at this point TMS equals MC and equal numbers divided by the same number are equal. The importance of this concept can be seen in Figure 4 where Bowen assumes that the individual demand curves will fall into a normal pattern of distribution. Assuming a normal distribution,

19. Individual cost shares can be determined in this manner only if it is a constant cost product, because in the other cases the revenue would not equal the total cost.

the average equals the mode. Therefore, the modal demand curve is the same as the average demand curve and its use results in the determination of the same "ideal" output as does the use of the total demand curve.

The assumption of the normal distribution is also important in the interpretation of the voting process made by Bowen, because if each individual votes on the quantity of the service he would desire, the

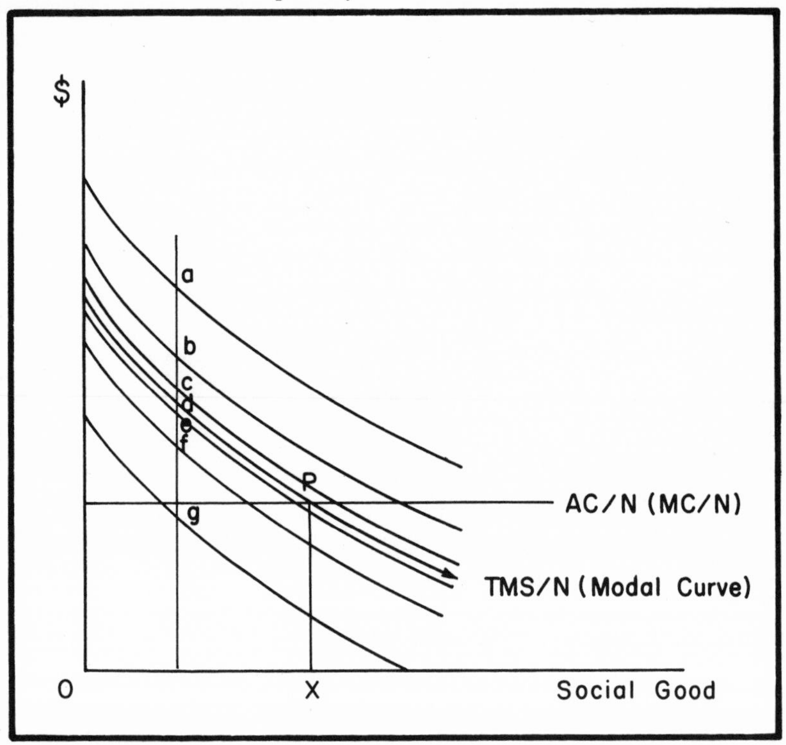

Figure 4.

"ideal" output is both the output which gets exactly one-half of the votes and that which gets more votes than any other quantity. In the case of voting on various increments or decrements to a given quantity of a social good, the "ideal" output is the one which gets exactly one half of the votes yes and one half no. Smaller quantities will receive a greater number of yes votes than the "ideal" output.

Three assumptions which are explicitly made by Bowen, and were implicit in the presentation, are important: (1) the income distribution is "correct" (i.e., the income distribution has been accepted by society; this is the necessary assumption in order to use price theory of private goods for a policy recommendation); (2) the product will be available equally to all individuals so that the differences in demand represent differences in tastes and preferences rather than just differences in benefits (a normal curve of distribution cannot be assumed if benefits are different to each individual voter); and (3) the cost of producing the product in various quantities is known to the voters and will be divided equally among the voters. This means that the voter automatically knows his cost (AC/N). In other words, the voter knows his relative share of the total expenditure of the social good.

The second and third assumptions can be modified by assuming that those receiving different benefits can be grouped into classes so that the members of each class do receive the same benefit[20] and that the costs will be distributed according to the modal demand for each class but that the individual and classes of individuals are not affected in their expressed demand by the fact that their demand affects their own relative cost share. Figure 5 presents Bowen's model.[21]

The relationship between the Lindahl model and the Bowen model is both interesting and important. Figure 6 presents another Bowen model like Figure 3 and another Lindahl model like Figure 1. The curves of the Lindahl model have been determined by the curves in the Bowen model. The total expenditure is computed by multiplying the quantity by the average cost (AC). The percentage of the total expenditure which each individual is willing to pay is computed by dividing the individual's demand by the total cost at each possible output. The output determined by moth models is the same. The assumption that average cost is constant is essential to the reconciliation of the two models because the equilibrium of the Lindahl model will occur at the output determined by the intersections of average cost and the total demand curve in the Bowen model. Another assumption which is necessary in the reconciliation of the two models is that the AR and BS curves of Figure 1 must be taken as demand curves of two individuals rather than of two groups of legislators. This is the interpretation of the Lindahl model used by Musgrave, but it ignores Lindahl's consideration of output being

20. An example can be made of education where one class of people have no children and the other classes can be listed by the number of children per family. Under these conditions, each classification of people can be assumed to have the same benefit and, therefore, it can reasonably be assumed that within each classification, tastes and preferences will vary in accordance with a normal distribution.

21. Bowen's model does not determine the tax-price. It is given by the MC/N curve assumed for each class.

determined in parliament. If the Lindahl model is interpreted to be two groups of legislators representing two classes of individuals in society, it would be necessary to assume that all individuals in each class have the same demand function or that all individual demands are vertically added and the individual cost shares are determined by the modal or average demand of the particular classes of society. The modal curves as developed by Bowen in Figure 5 cannot be used to reconcile the two

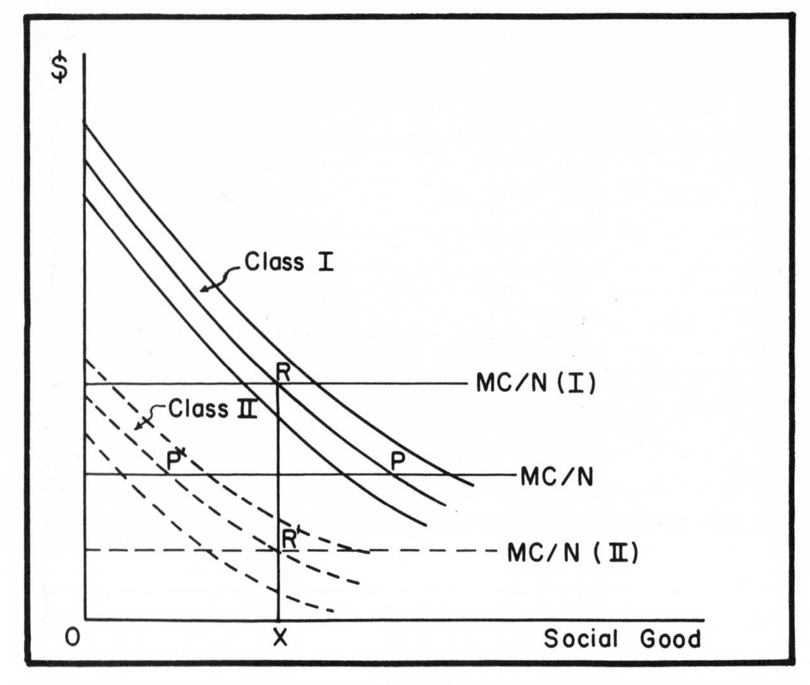

Figure 5.

models because Bowen has started with a given per-unit cost for each class of society. To look at it another way, the reconciliation requires two assumptions: (1) the individual demand curves are not affected by the fact that the expressed demand affects the relative cost shares of the individuals; and (2) the legislators have perfectly measured the total demand function of all individuals of society or the modal demand function of the individuals which the particular group of legislators represent.

Bowen's article also brings to light several other points of interest to the price theory of public finance. One point relates to the quantitative measurement of social goods. Bowen makes the point that some social goods like education cannot be measured in simple physical units of volume, time, or weight. Education consists of buildings, equipment, number of teachers, quality of teachers, etc.[22] Each of these components

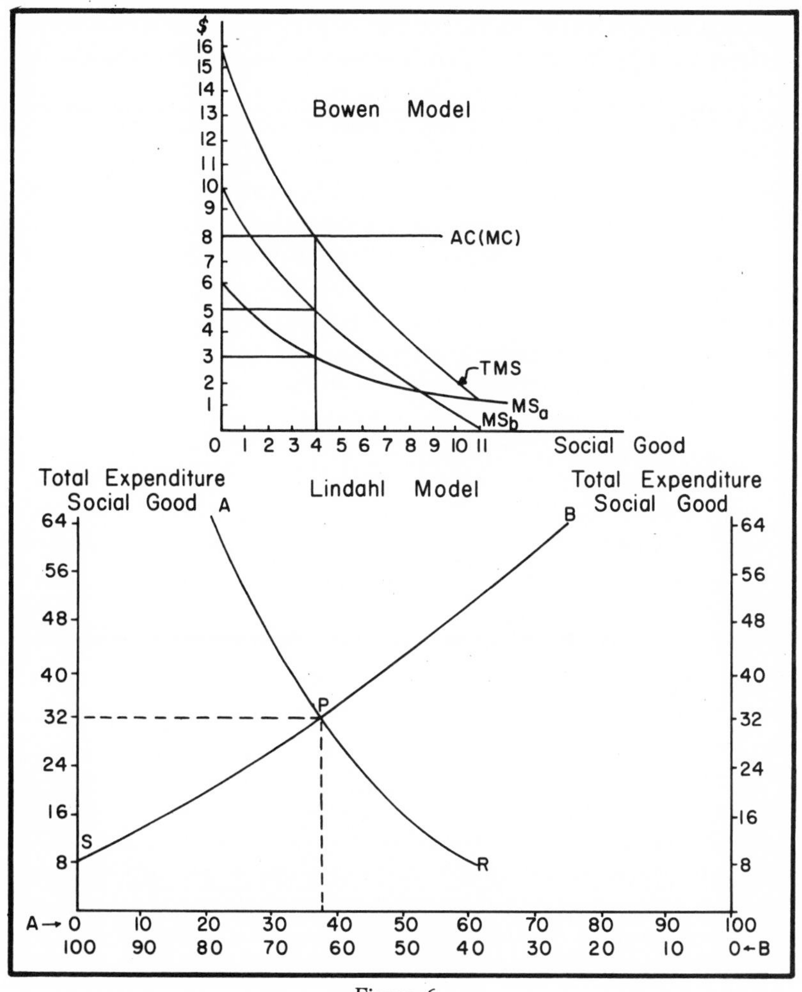

Figure 6.

22. Lindahl's concept of voting on all economically related goods at one time may be interpreted to mean the same thing, or it may be taken to mean goods related by tastes and preferences. In either case, Musgrave's criticisms of Lindahl, based on the concept that all goods which are capable of being determined by the benefit principle are lumped together in one vote, are not valid.

of education can be measured as separate goods and the theory applied to each. This, however, would only be realistic for a large item like buildings. However, to Bowen this does not rule out the use of the theory for education as a whole. Quantity can be measured by total expenditures on education if it is assumed that the voters have knowledge of an existing list of priorities.[23] In other words, if the voters know, or beforehand establish, the order in which expenditures will be made on the component parts of education, the quantity of education can be measured in terms of the total expenditure to be made on education.

These considerations of education made by Bowen point out the problem of not carrying out the concept of the price theory of public finance to its logical conclusions. Buildings, teachers, equipment, etc., are resources used to produce a product—education. The allocation of these resources should be based upon the least-cost distribution of resources and not the demand of individuals. Education must be measured in terms of levels of knowledge attained. In other words, the quantity of education which individuals compare with their cost in attempting to maximize their satisfaction is a quantity in terms of the level of education (eighth grade, high school, college degree, etc.) which individuals want the government to supply. It is clear that levels of education and levels of knowledge are not the same thing, even if the function of education is to provide knowledge, but it is reasonable to assume that individuals in our society do measure education in terms of levels of education.

Another important concept discussed by Bowen is the alternatives to voting. Recognizing that the individual voting process is not practical for any unit of government larger than that which can operate on a town-meeting basis, Bowen suggests the use by public officials of polls of random samples of society. "If a poll is based on a representative sample of the population and if the questions are put in the same way as if the entire citizenry were voting, the results could be interpreted in exactly the same way [as the vote of all the people]."[24] Bowen is quick to add that it would be necessary that those polled be well informed on the issue and be responsible citizens with a knowledge that their choices will influence policy. These two conditions might be difficult to meet and still have a representative sample of the entire voting

23. The concept and importance of establishing a list of priorities in expenditures was developed by Emil Sax; see Musgrave and Peacock, pp. 177-89, for translation of a part of Sax, *Die Wertungstheorie der Steuer* (1929).

24. Bowen, p. 43.

public, but it is a start in the direction of finding a means by which the political process (that in all modern societies must make the ultimate decision as to what and how much of social goods are to be produced by the government) can ascertain the individual demand for social goods.[25]

Milton Z. Kafoglis

In 1962 Milton Z. Kafoglis[26] added to the stock of theoretical models which were related back to the original Lindahl model.[27] Kafoglis' formulation makes use of a derivation of net demand curves for each individual based on the individual's recognition that the consumption of the social goods by other individuals gives him a "windfall" of satisfaction.

Kafoglis relates his net demand curve model to the concept of "cost of service pricing" and the Bowen vertical summation of demand curve model[28] to the concept of "value of service pricing."[29] To Kafoglis the "cost of service" concept involves a horizontal summation of adjusted (net) demand curves to arrive at the collective demand. The per-unit tax-price paid is the same to all individuals, as in the case of private goods without price discrimination. The taxpayer-consumer adjusts his consumption according to his adjusted (net) demand curve. The "value of service" concept, using a vertical summation of demand curves, results in different per-unit tax-prices being paid by different individuals, but with all individuals consuming the same units of production. The total cost to each individual and total production is shown by Kafoglis

25. The function of pressure groups in the modern democratic state may be somewhat similar to the process of polling a segment of the economy, if certain assumptions are made about the nature of the pressure groups and the extent of influence which the pressure groups have in the political process. More will be said about pressure groups in Chapter 4.

26. *Welfare Economics and Subsidy Programs.* Other models of recent years are in Buchanan, "Pure Theory of Government Finance," p. 496; Samuelson, "Diagrammatic Exposition of a Theory of Public Expenditures," p. 350; Tiebout, "Pure Theory of Local Expenditures," p. 416. The Samuelson model was used as a criticism of the voluntary exchange approach to public finance, and is reviewed in Chapter 3 (herein) to the extent that Musgrave used it as a means of presenting a comprehensive review and criticism of the theory.

27. Related to the Lindahl model if the latter is interpreted as a model of individual equilibrium rather than one of political equilibrium.

28. Kafoglis puts the Bowen model in terms of ordinary demand curves rather than marginal substitution curves.

29. E. Seligman, *Studies in Public Finance*, pp. 182-90, set forth the distinction between "cost of service pricing" and "value of service pricing," relating the former to the protection, and the latter to the benefit, theory of taxation.

to be the same in either case.[30] Therefore, it follows that the net demand curve analysis can be applied where the social good involves joint satisfaction but individual consumption, while the vertical summation of demand curve analysis must be applied where the social good has joint consumption (joint supply).

The derivation of the net demand curve makes use of indifference curve analysis and income consumption lines which are a familiar part of accepted price theory analysis. Figure 7 presents the indifference

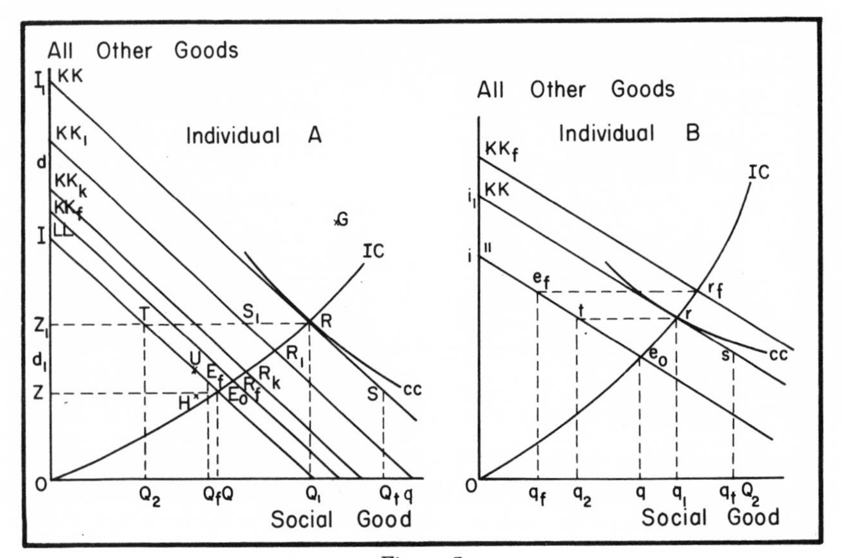

Figure 7.

maps of two individuals, A and B. The process of adjustment can be made by starting with either individual seeking equilibrium without the knowledge that the consumption of the other individual will affect the satisfaction derived from any given quantity of the social good consumed by the first individual, or by starting with both in an equilibrium position before the recognition of "windfall" satisfaction.

Assuming E_0 is the original equilibrium combination for A with income level LL, and e_0 for B with income level ll, the first step of adjustment takes place when A realizes that he has derived satisfaction from the quantity q purchased by B as well as the satisfaction derived from his own purchase of Q quantity of the social good. This additional

30. Kafoglis' proof of this point is based on the constant marginal cost model of Bowen and a simplified version of the net demand curve derived in detail later on.

satisfaction experienced by A results in a lowering of A's marginal rate of substitution for the social good. Graphically this can be presented by indicating the level of satisfaction received by A ($S = Q + q$). At this marginal rate of substitution A would want R combination of goods if he had I_1 income. Since he does not have this level of income, A will adjust his purchases to combination T and take Q_2 quantity of the social good instead of quantity Q. Individual B then recognizes that he received satisfaction from A's purchase of quantity Q_2 of the social good. Therefore, B's marginal rate of substitution for

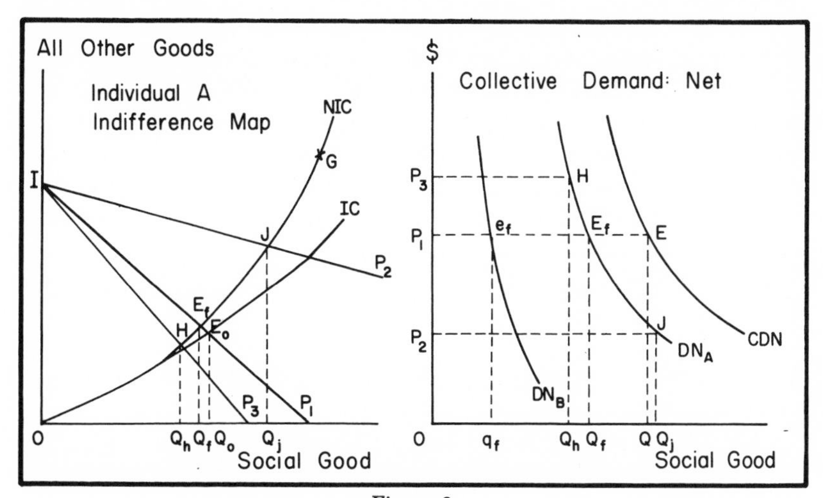

Figure 8.

the social good is reduced as shown by position s. Given B's income level ll, he will reduce his purchases of the social good to q_2 from q. This change, however, affects the satisfaction of A since A's purchases were based on B's consumption of quantity q of the social good. A's marginal rate of substitution for social goods has been increased by B's action. Therefore, A must increase his consumption of the social good to U in order to reach an equilibrium consistent with B's purchase of q_2 quantity of the social good. This action, however, alters the satisfaction obtained by B. B must, therefore, make another adjustment.

The result of the adjustment process is the establishment of an equilibrium at E_f for A and e_f for B. The level of satisfaction for B is r_f which is the satisfaction from Q_f and q consistent with B's original income consumption curve.

The starting income level can be changed and the process repeated.

Figure 7 for individual A indicates points H and G which are equilibrium combinations starting with a lower and a higher income than I. These equilibrium positions are carried over to Figure 8 where a "Net Income Consumption" curve is indicated. The net curve reflects a change in the indifference map resulting from the recognition of joint satisfaction on the part of individual A. Based on the net income consumption curve, a demand schedule can be established which also takes into consideration the joint satisfaction derived from the social good. Again assuming I level of income for A, the price of the social good can be varied (P_3, P_1, and P_2). The quantities Q_h, Q_f, and Q_j are determined. These price and quantity relationships are a part of A's net demand schedule (DN_A); e_f is an equilibrium combination for individual B. The balance of B's net demand curve (DN_B) can be derived in the same manner as A's. The two curves can then be horizontally summed to determine the "Net Collective Demand" (CDN). Assuming a constant cost social good, with AC and MC equal to P_1, the total output would be Q and both A and B would pay P_1. A would take Q_f and B would take q_f.

Kafoglis' formulation is of particular importance because it points out the distinction and importance of the two types of external economies of consumption; joint satisfaction and joint consumption (joint supply). The Lindahl and Bowen models involve goods which have the characteristic of joint consumption (joint supply). The Kafoglis model involves a good which has the characteristic of joint satisfaction. The methodology used in analysis must be consistent with the particular characteristic of the public good which gives rise to the situation where external economies of consumption do exist. This also implies that when a particular methodology is used, the good in the analysis could be discussed in terms of the characteristic with which the methodology is consistent.

3. REVEALED PREFERENCES

There are two basic criticisms of the voluntary exchange theory of public finance involving revealed preferences. The first states that the individual will not reveal his true preferences for public goods. The second is that even if the individual did reveal his true preferences for a public good, there is no single solution to the problem of allocating resources analogous to that found in the allocation of resources to private goods. Both criticisms have been raised by Richard A. Musgrave and have apparently been accepted by many economists. In fact, although Musgrave was one of the first to bring the voluntary exchange or price theory of public finance to the attention of American economists, he was also one of its strongest critics and has led the way to the rejection of the theory.[1]

The first criticism was raised by Musgrave in relation to Lindahl's model. As it relates specifically to the Lindahl model, the criticism was treated in Chapter 2. However, it may be taken as a more general criticism about the applicability of the price theory of public finance to the problem of allocating resources to any good which has the characteristic of joint consumption. Therefore, the first section of this chapter analyzes the criticism as it applies to the allocation of resources, without reference to any particular formulation of the price theory of public finance.

The second criticism is raised by Musgrave in relation to the applicability of the theory in a general equilibrium framework. Therefore, the general equilibrium model which was adopted by Musgrave to state the criticism is presented in the second section. The model is also applied to two private goods in order to determine whether it is the allocation of resources to a public good with joint consumption which is not analogous to the allocation of resources to private goods, or whether it is the model used in the Musgrave analysis which is not analogous to the theory of the allocation of resources to private goods.

Critique of the First Criticism

The question of whether or not preferences will be revealed by individuals for a public good through the political process is both a practical and a theoretical consideration. The theoretical issue is whether or

1. See *Theory of Public Finance;* and "Voluntary Exchange Theory."

not there is something inherent in the nature of public goods or in the supply of and demand for public goods which makes it necessary or likely that the individual acting rationally would not reveal his preferences for the public goods. One situation that might lead to such a conclusion is one in which an individual can derive satisfaction from the supply of a public good without having to express a

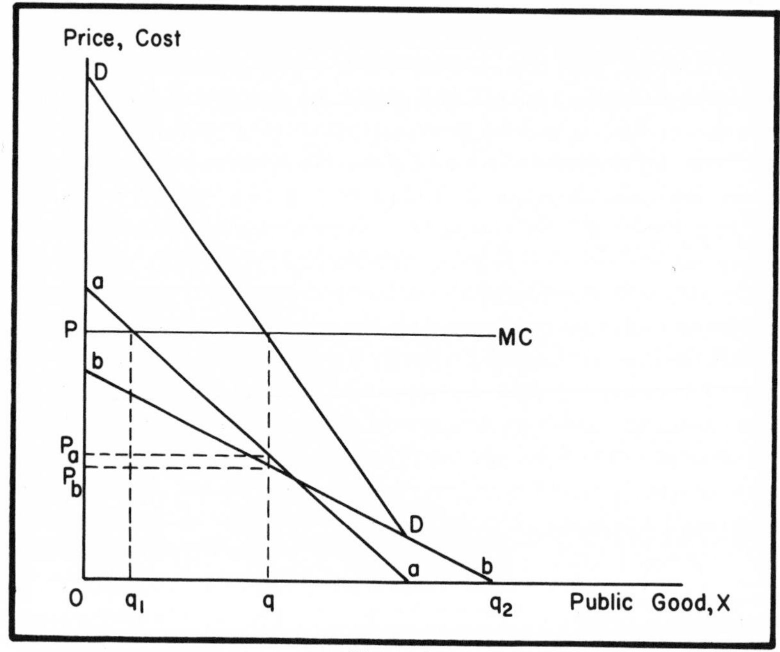

Figure 9.

desire for the good and without having to pay for the good according to his actual individual satisfaction. Musgrave's attempt to illustrate such a situation is based on two propositions: (1) an equal quantity of public goods and services is consumed by all taxpayer-buyers; (2) an individual taxpayer's demand exerts no influence over the quantity of public goods supplied.[2]

The first proposition involves a problem of defining a public good in terms of its characteristics. The public good is said to be a good which has the characteristic that each individual receives benefits from the entire supply as if he were the only individual consuming it (i.e., joint consumption). The equal-consumption definition of a public good

2. *Theory of Public Finance.*

is accepted as a polar case which is possible even if it may not exist for many goods.[3] The issue here is whether or not a good which does fit this definition is likely to be the cause of individuals not revealing their preferences for the good.

Figure 9 presents one possible formulation of the process through which preferences might be revealed even when the equal-consumption definition is accepted and when each individual pays according to his revealed preferences.[4] There are two taxpayers A and B. If taxpayers A and B reveal their true preferences, a vertical summation of their individual demands (aa and bb) would be designated by DD. The optimum amount of public good X, then, is Oq, and the optimum distribution of the costs of producing good X is $OP_a \cdot Oq$ for taxpayer A and $OP_b \cdot Oq$ for taxpayer B. Assume that taxpayer A reveals his true preferences and that taxpayer B does not reveal his preferences. The collective demand is only A's demand (aa) and only Oq_1 of good X will be made available for equal consumption. Taxpayer A is in equilibrium but taxpayer B is not. If B's tax share is zero, as it would be if B does not reveal any preference for X, B really desires Oq_2 of X at the existing zero price instead of the quantity Oq_1 which will be made available. Therefore, taxpayer B may have an inclination to reveal at least some of his preferences. If B reveals part of his preferences, his tax share of the Oq_1 of X rises above zero and A's tax share declines. At the lower price to A (OP — B's price), A demands a greater quantity of X. The process, followed to its logical conclusions, results in a situation where both A and B do reveal their true preferences.

Musgrave's second proposition involves the question of the effect that having a large number of individuals participate in the determination of what quantity should be produced will have upon a single individual's revealing his preferences. In Chapter 2, Musgrave's analysis was rejected. The rejection of the duopoly type of analysis was not based on the use of small numbers in the analysis, but on the assumption that the individual bargained with other individuals as if he were a producer attempting to maximize his profits. The individual who has preferences for goods is a consumer, not a producer. Therefore, the

3. A great deal of discussion was created, as to whether or not the equal-consumption definition had any application in the real world, after Samuelson used it in his model as a polar case ("Diagrammatic Exposition").

4. Sharp and Escarraz, "Reconsideration of the Price or Exchange Theory of Public Finance."

analysis must be based upon the individual's attempting to maximize his satisfaction. Thus, it is necessary to assume that the individual does have preferences in regard to public goods, or that he does receive satisfaction from public goods in relation to the quantities he consumes. The latter will be assumed in the analysis which follows, so that simple mathematical expression of the assumption of maximization of satisfaction in terms of marginal utilities may be used.[5]

If the individual derives satisfaction from each public good as he does from each private good, the maximization of satisfaction would be expressed exactly the same for both private and public goods $\left(\frac{MU_a}{T_a} = \frac{MU_b}{T_b} = \cdots \frac{MU_y}{P_y} = \frac{MU_z}{P_z}\right)$. The goods represented by a and b can be taken as public goods, such as national defense and education, and the goods represented by y and z can be taken as private goods, such as automobiles and fountain pens.

Given this type of maximization of satisfaction criterion, it would be impossible for the individual to maximize his satisfaction if one of the goods has equal consumption and if at the same time everybody must pay the same price. The tax-price and the quantity supplied cannot both be the same for all individuals unless it is assumed that each individual has the same utility function for the good. Therefore, the individual under these conditions would have no reason to reveal his preferences for the public good.

However, if the tax-price is permitted to vary between individuals and if it is determined by the tastes and preferences of the individual (i.e., in accordance with the benefit theory of taxation), he can maximize his satisfaction. The fact that one of the goods has equal consumption does not interfere with the individual's ability to maximize his satisfaction. In fact, the quantity of the public good which is supplied does not have to be based upon the tastes and preferences of individuals just so long as the individual's tax-price is determined by the individual's preference for the given quantity.[6] Therefore, the individual un-

5. The acceptance of indifference-curve analysis and relative diminishing marginal utility between two goods instead of marginal-utility analysis and absolute diminishing marginal utility for all goods does not affect the conclusions about revealed preferences which follow.

6. The fact that the quantity of the public good is not based upon the tastes and preferences of individuals does affect the allocation of resources, but it does not affect the individual's ability to maximize his satisfaction or his motivation to reveal his preferences. More is said about the effect of this type of situation on the allocation of resources in Chapter 5.

der these conditions would have a motivation to reveal his preferences for the public good.

The fact that a large number of individuals might be involved is significant under the foregoing analysis only as a practical consideration. The individual maximizing his satisfaction is not affected by the number of other individuals attempting to maximize theirs except as the number of individuals affects the government's ability to base the tax-price on the individual's tastes and preferences.[7]

Another practical consideration, however, should be made at this point. The analysis assumed that the individual knows his tax-price will be based upon his tastes and preferences for each public good. If it is assumed that the individual accepts the total of government activity as one public good, it would not be necessary to assume that the tax-price is based upon the individual's tastes and preferences for each good supplied by the government.[8] The maximization of satisfaction criterion becomes $\frac{MU_g}{T_g} = \cdot \cdot \cdot = \frac{MU_y}{P_y} = \frac{MU_z}{P_z}$. In this case g represents all government activity and T_g represents the individual's average tax bill per unit of government goods and services. The allocation of resources to particular public goods, such as national defense, highways, education, etc., would have to be based upon the least-cost combination of these goods in providing various quantities of the good — total government activity.

Given this type of maximization criterion, it would be possible for the individual to maximize his satisfaction. This follows even if the good, total government activity, is assumed to have the characteristic of equal consumption and if the tax-price is not based upon the individual's tastes and preferences. In this case, the individual's $\frac{MU_g}{T_g}$ is determined independent of his tastes and preferences. The individual maximizes his satisfaction by adjusting his private consumption.[9] Pref-

7. The effect of various types of organizations upon the applicability of the voluntary exchange or price theory of public finance is treated in Chapter 4.

8. DeViti DeMarco states a belief that as the practice of special assessment decreases, "the taxpayer, in making up his own budget no longer compares every special assessment with the consumption of the corresponding service but compares the whole of his taxes with the whole of the services he consumes" (*First Principles of Public Finance*, p. 110).

9. In accepted price theory of private goods the adjustment takes place solely as a result of the decreased income available for private consumption. In the above formulation of the price theory of public goods, income available for private consumption is reduced by the same process, but the individual's private consumption is restricted still further by the necessity of making his marginal

erences for public goods are revealed but the revealing process must be done through the adjustment of private consumption.[10]

However, if the goverment does attempt to base the tax-price upon individual tastes and preferences (the benefit principle of taxation), the individual will be able to maximize his satisfaction by adjusting his tax-price as an alternative to adjusting his private consumption. Therefore the individual may have a motivation to reveal his preferences for total government activity through the political process.

In either case, preferences are revealed. In the one case, the assumption about the nature of the political process makes it necessary for the individual to reveal his preferences through his behavior in the market process. If the political process is capable of basing taxes upon individual tastes and preferences, the individual has a motivation to reveal his preferences for the public good in the political process.

Critique of the Second Criticism

Assuming true preferences are revealed, Musgrave contends that there is still another flaw in the voluntary exchange theory model. "Even if all preferences are revealed, there is no single best solution analogous to the Pareto optimum in the satisfaction of purely private wants. Instead we are confronted with large number of solutions, all of which are optimal in the Pareto sense."[11]

The equilibrium model used by Musgrave to derive these conclusions is based upon a model developed by Samuelson.[12] Figure 10 is a reproduction of the Musgrave version of this model. The bottom diagram is the familiar transformation curve, and the other two are indifference maps of individuals A and B. OC and OD are said to represent the distribution of income between A and B, since OC and OD are the quantities of private goods they could hold if they held only private goods with their income. Individual A is arbitrarily moved along his indifference curve i_1, which contains combination OC of private goods. Given the transformation curve's production limits, this process limits individual B to a specific combination of social and private goods for

utility per dollar's worth of spending for each private good equal to the arbitrarily determined marginal utility per dollar's worth of spending for public goods.

10. Tiebout presents still another means of revealing preferences when he concludes from his analysis that preferences for local government services are expressed by individuals through their choice of suburban community around the large cities in our modern society ("Pure Theory of Local Expenditures").

11. *Theory of Public Finance*, p. 84.

12. *Ibid.*, p. 81n.

each point on individual A's indifference curve. Curve MD, therefore, represents the various combinations of public and private goods available to individual B as individual A is arbitrarily moved along his indifference curve i_1. Point W is the point of tangency with the highest possible indifference curve and determines the quantities OG of public

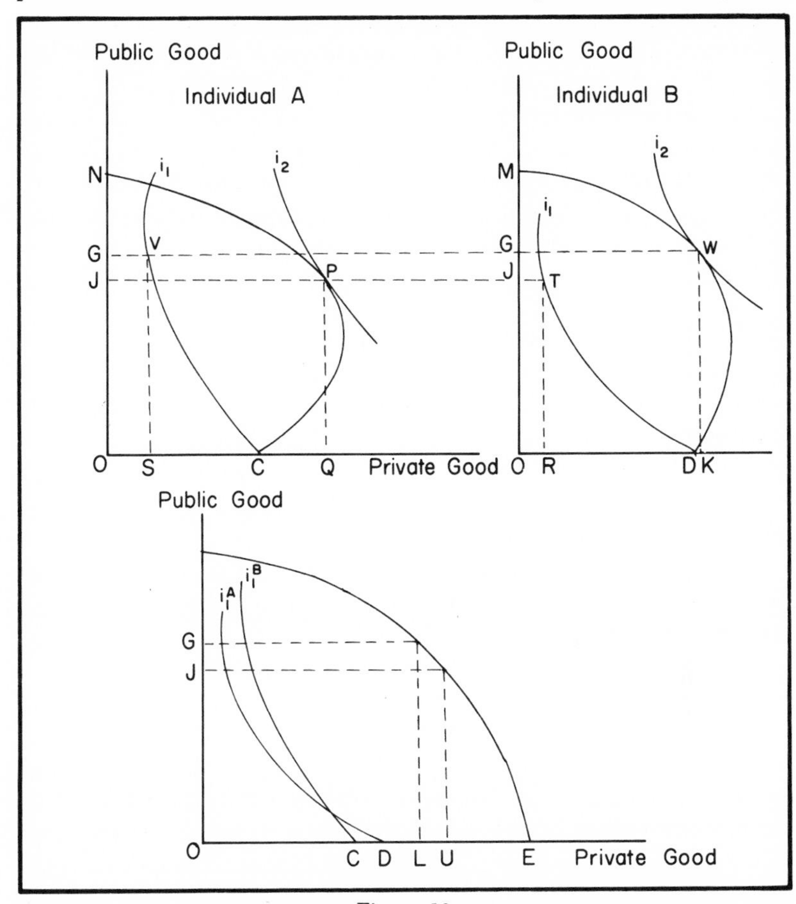

Figure 10.

goods and OK of private goods which individual B would desire without individual A being worse off than if he held all of his income as private goods. The same process is then followed for individual A by moving individual B along his indifference curve i_1. Curve NC is then developed and quantities OJ of public goods and OQ of private goods are found to be the combination individual A would desire without making individual B worse off than if he held all his income in private goods.[13]

The optima developed in the foregoing analysis are presented on a utility frontier (Figure 11). Point X represents the ordinal measurement of satisfaction for individuals A and B when individual A has the

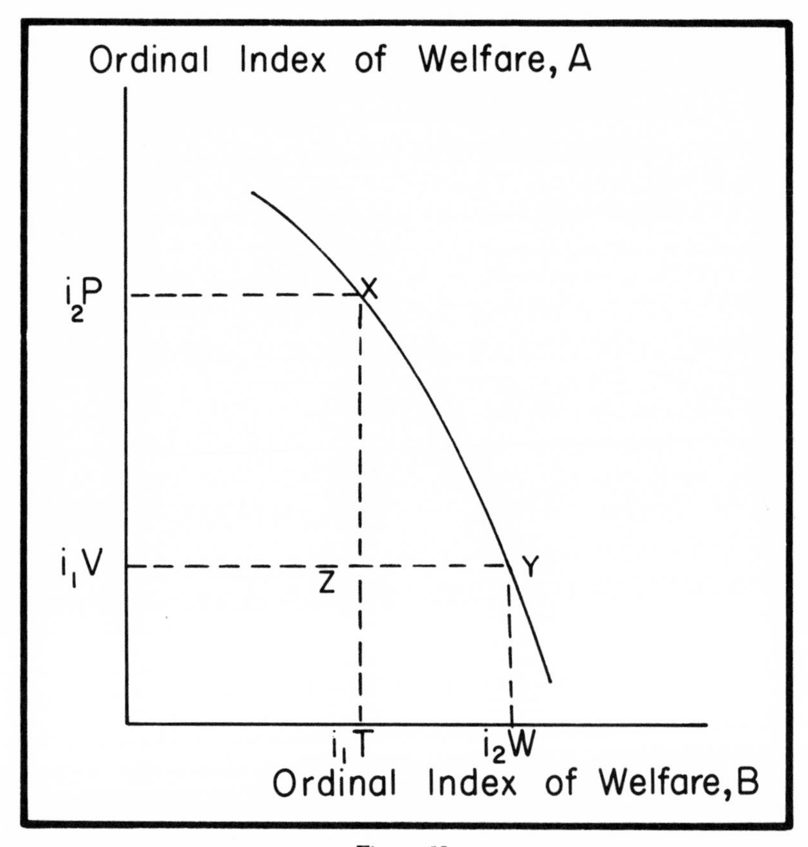

Figure 11.

13. Musgrave assumes that the distribution of income is given and does not change but this is incompatible with the methodology used. If we consider it a general equilibrium view with only two goods and two individuals, the distribution of the physical units represents the income distribution. Figure B shows that the one solution resulted in individual A holding OQ of the private good and individual B holding OR of the private good and the two holding OJ of the public good. The other solution gave individual A, OS of the private good and individual B, OK of the private good and both individuals had OG of the public good. It, therefore, does not appear to be correct to say that the distribution of income remains OC/OE for individual A and OD/OE for individual B.

combination P and individual B has the combination T of public and private goods. Point Y represents the ordinal measurement of satisfaction when individual A has the combination V and individual B has the combination W of public and private goods. The other points on the utility frontier could be developed by varying the original distribution of income so that either or both individuals are on a different indifference curve at the start of the analysis. The conclusion drawn from the analysis is that "the area ZYX [in Figure 11] shows the infinite number of possible solutions that leave A, B or both, better off than at Z, where no public services are supplied."[14]

The above review of the methodology used by Musgrave raises the question of whether the arbitrary movement of one individual along an indifference curve, to determine what combination of goods a second individual would like to hold, is compatible with price theory analysis. The "Edgeworth box analysis" of exchange makes use of this method to establish a contract curve which contains an infinite number of optima. In other words, it establishes those changes in social variables which can take place through "trading."[15]

Trading, however, is not the object of the voluntary payments model. The voluntary exchange approach must be based upon a money economy and not a barter economy. The Musgrave analysis tells us nothing more than what the "Edgeworth box analysis" tells. In other words, it is the barter nature of the analysis (i.e., the arbitrary holding of one individual on a given indifference curve while permitting the other to choose the combination of goods which maximizes his satisfaction) which causes the existence of an infinite number of Pareto optima points.

Figure 12 presents the Musgrave analysis using the private good definition for both goods. The change in definition does cause a basic change in the procedure. This change is that the placing of individual A at a point on his indifference curve leaves a line of attainable combinations (based upon the price ratios set by the transformation curve) available to individual B instead of a specific combination of the two goods. Assuming the individuals maximize their satisfaction, we can still determine the one combination which individual B will hold when individual A is at each point on his given indifference curve. Therefore, we can still determine a curve MD_1, which is analogous to the MD

14. Musgrave, *Theory of Public Finance*, pp. 83-84.

15. Kenneth E. Boulding, "Welfare Economics," in American Economic Association Committee, *Survey of Contemporary Economics*, pp. 18-19.

curve found with one good defined as a public good. Using arbitrary movements along individual B's indifference curve, we can determine individual A's NC_1 curve which is analogous to the NC curve found with the public good definition. The combination of private goods 1 and 2 which individual A could hold without making individual B worse off

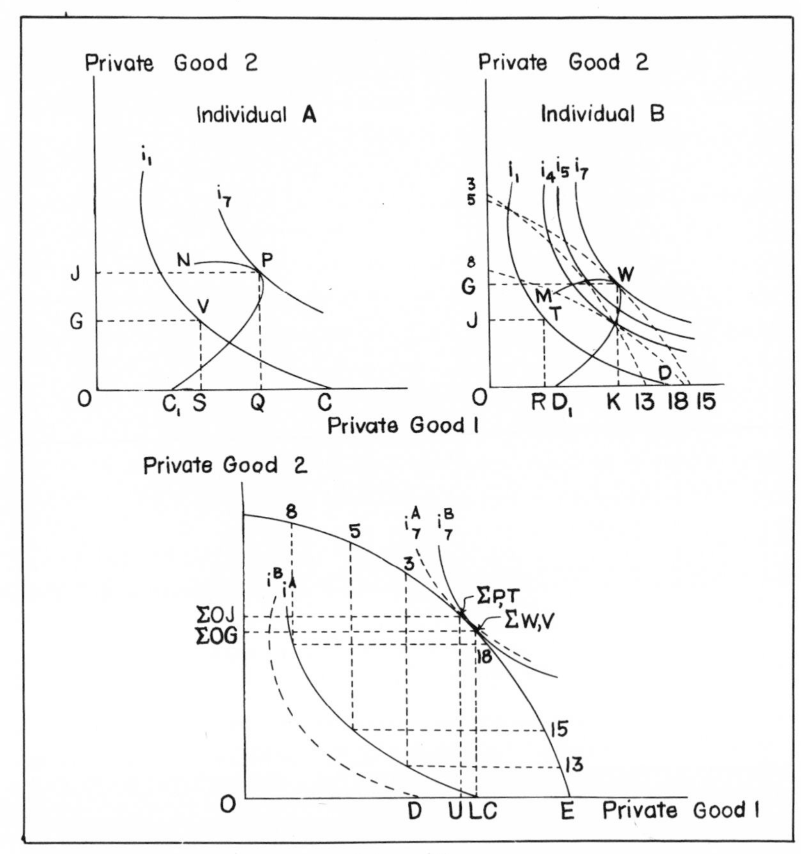

Figure 12.

is OQ and OJ, respectively. Individual B could hold OG of private good 2 and OK of private good 1 without making individual A worse off.

The optima developed in the analysis with two private goods can be presented on a utility frontier (Figure 13). Points X and Y have the same meaning as points X and Y in Figure 11, except that now we are considering the quantity of two private goods to be supplied. The area ZYX shows the infinite number of possible solutions that leave A, B, or both better off than at Z, where no quantity of private good 2 would be supplied.

It has been shown that the model used by Musgrave results in an infinite number of optima when a public good and a private good are used or when two private goods are used. Any conclusion derived from

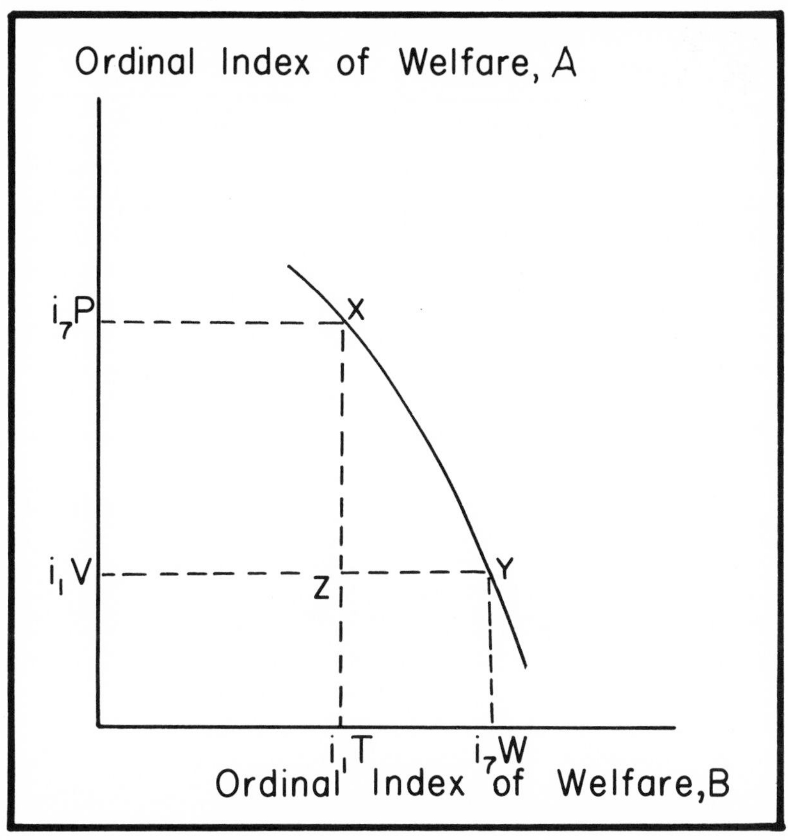

Figure 13.

Musgrave's model is applicable to price theory in general. Musgrave is correct when he concludes from his public goods model that a single optimum cannot be reached. However, it appears that the absence of a single optimum solution is not due to the inclusion of a public good in the model. The rejection of the criticism is based on the fact that the model used by Musgrave to prove the validity of the criticism is not consistent with the price theory of private goods, and therefore could not be expected to yield a single optimum when applied to public goods.

Samuelson did originate the model and did criticize the voluntary exchange approach to public finance in the same article.[16] The criticisms, however, were in terms of whether or not preferences would be revealed and the model was in terms of a solution to the problem. Although Musgrave and other economists appeared to believe that the cause of the large number of solutions in the model was the existence of a public good with the characteristic of joint consumption, Samuelson never made such a statement. In fact, Samuelson in developing his model refers to his original work on an exchange model in *Foundations.* In this original exchange model the goods are not assumed to have the characteristic of joint consumption, and yet his conclusion is that "Because the original specification of the second man's utility was arbitrary, the final equilibrium is also arbitrary and not unique."[17] The statement was made with respect to the "Edgeworth box analysis," but in fact the Samuelson model is nothing more than a presentation of Edgeworthian analysis where the quantity of goods is not fixed but is limited to the various quantities that could be produced under the conditions of efficiency. The existence of the public good in the model modifies the analysis but does not affect the nature of the conclusions. The arbitrary statement of the second man's utility is the cause of the large number of solutions in the model, and not the nature of the goods used in the model.

Samuelson solved the problem of a large number of solutions by using a welfare function for society. The traditional solution to an Edgeworthian analysis, however, is usually stated in terms of the relative bargaining powers of the individuals involved in the exchange. Price theory follows this traditional frame of reference in that income derived from the productivity of resources used in production determines the bargaining power of the individuals involved in the exchange. In the next chapter an attempt is made to convert the Musgrave-Samuelson model from a pure exchange model which requires a welfare function or an arbitrary statement of bargaining power of individuals to a model which rests on the principles of price theory.

16. "Pure Theory of Public Expenditure."
17. *Foundations of Economic Analysis*, p. 238.

4. A SUGGESTED APPROACH

Musgrave's criticism that there is no single optimum with respect to the voluntary exchange theory of public finance was rejected because the methodology used was not consistent with price theory analysis. It does not provide a single optimum when only private goods are used in the model. However, the Samuelson general equilibrium framework used by Musgrave has some merit. The problem is to modify the Musgrave-Samuelson model so that it is consistent with price theory general equilibrium anaylsis. The modified model then can be used with the restriction of a public good that has the characteristic of joint consumption in order to further evaluate the criticism of the voluntary exchange theory of public finance. The modified model may also be considered as a new approach to the presentation of the theory, which makes explicit some of its seldom stated conditions.

The Transformation Curve

The Musgrave-Samuelson model starts with a given transformation curve. This curve is based upon the production possibilities of firms producing the two classes of goods in the limited society of the model. By assuming that one firm, or that one group of firms with identical production functions, produces each of the two goods, derivation of the transformation curve can be shown graphically.[1] It is assumed that all of the existing (given)[2] resources will be used in the production process, and the determination of which firms will use the resources is to be determined on the basis of efficiency. It is also assumed, as in the case of Walrasian general equilibrium analysis, that the original distribution of ownership of resources is known (given).[3]

The combinations of X and Y (private good products) indicated by the transformation curve in Figure 15 are derived from the points of tangency of isoquants in Figure 14. These points of tangency indicate

1. Bator, "Simple Analytics of Welfare Maximization," pp. 3-24.

2. If the quantity of resources is not given, the transformation curve cannot be determined.

3. If the original ownership of resources is not given, there is no single best solution because the distribution of income in a market society depends upon the ownership of resources at the beginning of the productive process. This does not mean that the distribution of income is given. It is determinable with a market society and a given original distribution of ownership of resources.

the combinations of A and B (resources) that would be used by the firms producing products X and Y under the efficiency condition that $\frac{MPP^X_A}{MPP^X_B} = \frac{MPP^Y_A}{MPP^Y_B}$.

In a market society even more can be said from the simple derivation of the transformation curve. Under the conditions of pure competition in resource markets and in product markets, the ratio of the marginal productivities of the resources will also be equal to the ratio of

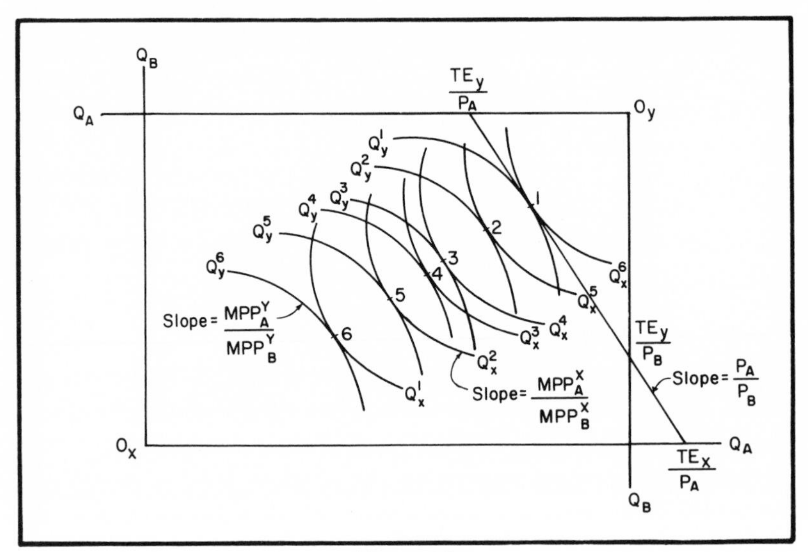

Figure 14.

the prices paid to the resources; $\frac{MPP^X_A}{MPP^X_B} = \frac{P_A}{P_B} = \frac{MPP^Y_A}{MPP^Y_B}$.[4] Since the quantity of A and B is given (Figure 14) and the ownership of A and B is assumed to be known, the ratio of prices paid to the resources determines the distribution of income. The level of money income is still indeterminate, but the distribution of any money income level among the owners of the resources is determined.

The transformation curve, under the conditions of pure competition in the product markets, determines another important condition for equilibrium in the market-price theory model. The slope of the transformation curve is the ratio of the marginal costs of producing the two goods

4. Bator (pp. 31-32) recognizes this point but does not assume that the original distribution of the ownership of resources is known and thus does not carry the analysis further.

($\frac{MC_X}{MC_Y}$). Since, under pure competition market conditions, the price of the product is equal to the marginal cost of producing the product, the transformation curve also determines the ratio of the prices of the products ($\frac{P_X}{P_Y}$).[5] This fixes the relationship of the value of X to Y but not the level of the money value of production. The combination of X and Y indicated by point 1 in Figure 15 cannot be an equilibrium solution under the conditions of pure competition. Given the production

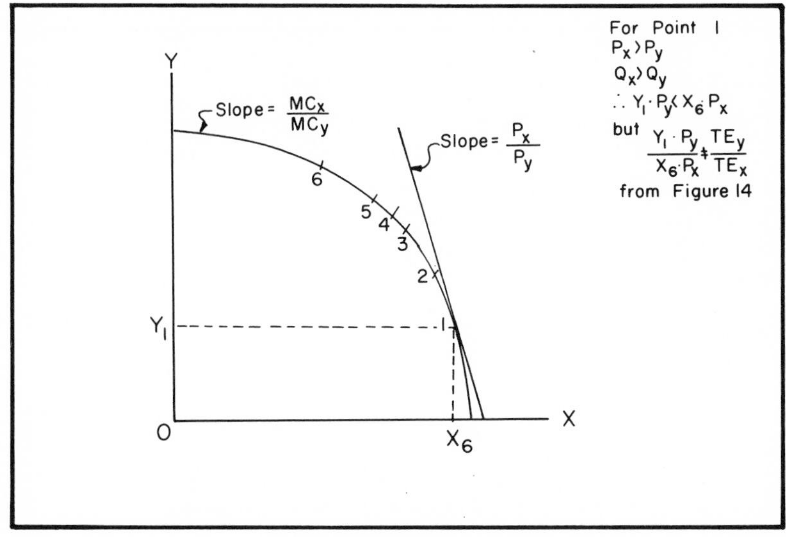

Figure 15.

of X and Y and the relationship of price between X and Y, the relationship of the expenditures by firms X and Y is determined. This determined relationship of expenditures for point 1 is, however, inconsistent with the relationship of expenditures indicated in Figure 14. The inconsistency can be seen more clearly if the analysis is carried further to consider the demand side of the picture.[6]

Demand Analysis

The distribution of income but not the level of money income was determined in Figure 14 for each combination of X and Y that might

5. Bator, pp. 32-33.

6. Bator works backwards from this point to show how exchange would take place with the determined relationship of value between X and Y. His solution, however, would require that revenue from one firm be redistributed to the other firm or that one firm operate at a loss.

be produced under the conditions of efficient production (i.e., for each point on the transformation curve). Under the simple assumption that all of resource A is owned by individual A and that all of resource B is owned by individual B, and the determined price ratio of the products from Figure 15, the lines of attainable combinations can be shown for the two individuals. There are a large number of such lines of attainable combinations for each efficiency output, depending upon the absolute prices paid for resources A and B, as is shown in Figure 16 for

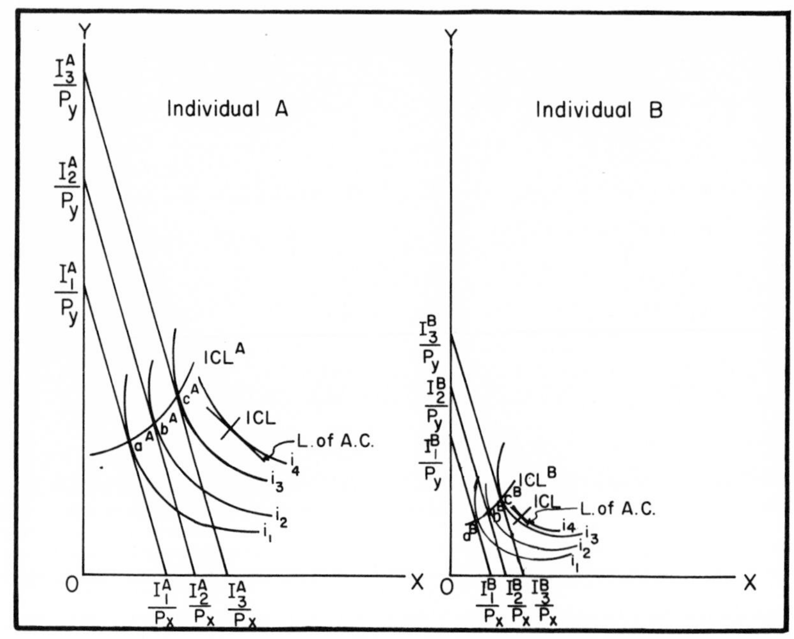

Figure 16.

point 1 and the transformation curve. Given the tastes and preferences for X and Y by individuals A and B, the points of tangency between the various lines of attainable combinations and the indifference curves determine the individuals' demand for products X and Y at the different money income levels. Demands a^A and a^B can be summed to obtain the total demand. The summing of the various demands for X and Y at different money incomes can be shown as a summation of individual income consumption lines and can be superimposed on the transformation curve diagram (Figure 17). The fact that the line of the sum of the income consumption lines does not intersect the transformation curve at the point 1 combination of X and Y indicates that there is no level of money income with the distribution of income determined by producing point 1 combination of X and Y under conditions of pure competition which will equate the demand and supply for products X and Y. Therefore, the combination of X and Y indicated by point 1 under the conditions of pure competition can only be an equilibrium solution if one of the firms is subsidized and the distribution of income is different from that which is provided by the market.

With the traditional assumptions of price theory analysis there will

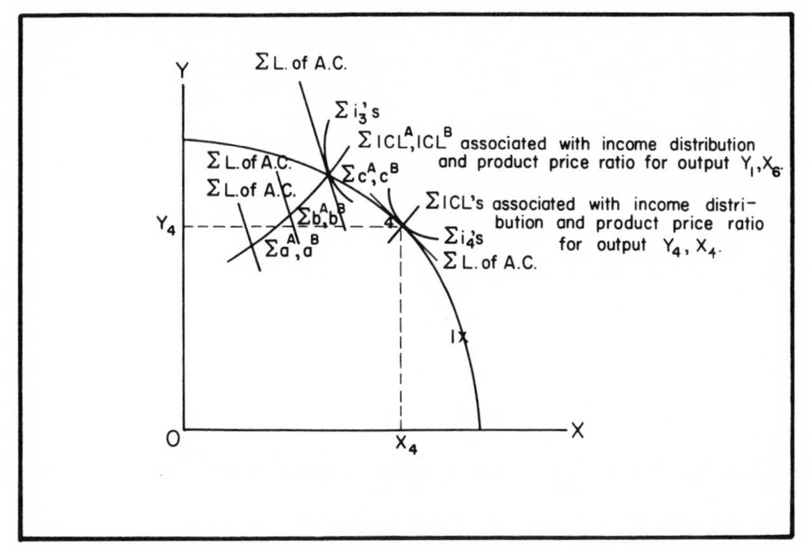

Figure 17.

be only one combination of X and Y which can be produced efficiently and which will be demanded when the distribution of income is determined by the productivity of the resources used to produce X and Y. (Again it should be noted that pure competition is assumed in both the product and the resource markets and the original ownership of the resources is known.) Figure 17 also shows this unique solution as well as the inconsistency between demand and supply which exists for one of the other combinations of X and Y.

Another approach to the problem can be presented in terms of the demand for product X and for product Y. In the above analysis the price ratio was given by the slope of the transformation curve. This price ratio is the only one which is consistent with the assumptions made about the markets involved. However, the price ratio is just the price of each good at equilibrium and a demand curve for both goods still exists. Thus instead of using income consumption lines the analysis could be based upon price consumption lines. Figure 18 shows

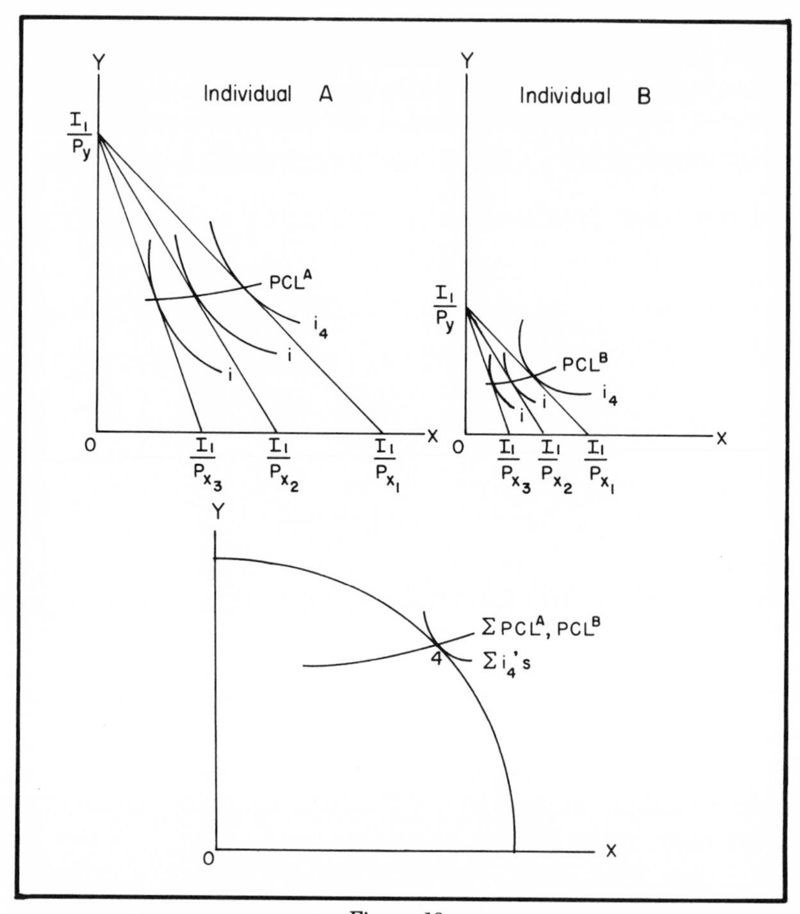

Figure 18.

the usual development of price consumption lines for the two individuals A and B. These individual price consumption lines are summed (i.e., the combination of X and Y desired by A with the same given price of X and Y is added to the combination of X and Y desired by B with the same given price of X and Y). The point where the summed price consumption line intersects the transformation curve gives a possible equilibrium. Whether or not it is an equilibrium solution under conditions of pure competition can be checked by summing the indifference curves of the two individuals. If the summed indifference curve is tangent to the transformation curve at the point where the summed price consumption line intersects the transformation curve, it is an equilibrium solution. The distribution of income must be given in order to use price demand analysis, but this is no problem since the income distribution was determined. In fact, as developed earlier, the equilibrium solution is known before the analysis is started. The price demand analysis merely adds one more consideration. It is an

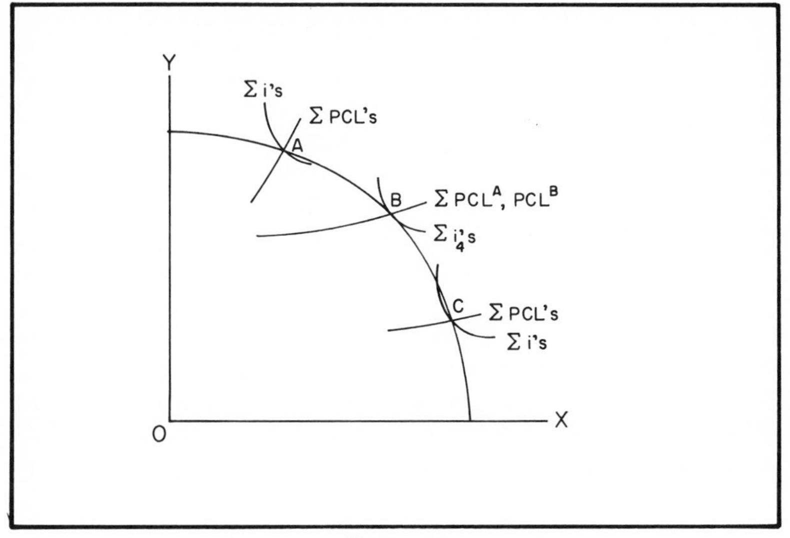

Figure 19.

important consideration later when the model is used with one private and one public good.

The single "best" solution derived in Figure 18 does assume that pure competition exists in both resource and in both product markets. If pure competition does not exist in the markets of both products, the Pareto optimum will not be achieved because there is no market force to cause the ratio of prices to be equal to the ratio of marginal costs (i.e., the slope of the line of attainable combinations would not have to equal the slope of the transformation curve at equilibrium). Figure 19 shows the three possible situations. Point A indicates a situation where the price of X is greater than the marginal cost of producing X. Point

C indicates a situation where the price of Y is greater than the marginal cost of producing Y.[7] Point B indicates the Pareto optimum presented in Figure 18. It is apparent that there are an infinite number of solutions, depending upon the specific market situations which might exist.[8] However, it is only when pure competition exists that the line of the sum of the individual price consumption lines intersects the transformation curve at a point where the curve of the sum of the individual indifference curves is tangent to the tranformation curve. When any other type of market situation exists in the product market of either good, the price of the good is greater than the marginal cost. Therefore, the ratio of prices (i.e., the slope of the attainable combinations and the slope of the individual indifference curves when the individual maximizes satisfaction) cannot equal the ratio of marginal costs. It should also be noted that the income distribution has not been altered even though the slope of the line of attainable combination is different from the slope of the transformation curve. In other words, if the ratio of prices does not have to equal the ratio of marginal costs, the income distribution does not determine a unique equilibrium. It would also be difficult to show graphically that the "correct" distribution of income has been maintained. The relative value of the two goods is different if pure competition does not exist. The supply of the good sold under conditions other than pure competition is restricted, and its price is higher than it would have been if pure competition had existed. Also excess profits will exist and would have to be distributed in some manner. Therefore, the absence of pure competition may create an income feedback problem and there may be no equilibrium solution. An equilibrium solution may exist but it need not exist because of the distribution of the excess profits in the system.

Demand Analysis with a Public Good

The changes necessary in the model to consider a public good with the characteristic of joint consumption are minor. The existence of an equilibrium is not changed, even though the equilibrium level is changed.[9] The distribution is still determined by the original owner-

7. In both situations it is assumed that the price of the other good in the situation is equal to the marginal costs of producing the good.

8. The infinite number of solutions here are not the same as those which exist in the Musgrave-Samuelson model. There, a specific solution depends upon the bargaining power of the individuals because it involves a barter exchange of goods. In this modified model a specific solution depends upon the market situations which are assumed to exist in the market economy.

9. The difference in the two equilibriums is the topic of the next section.

ship of the resources and the prices paid to the owners of resources based upon their use in the production of the two goods. The government can be assumed to purchase the resources they use under the conditions of pure competition in the resource market. The other assump-

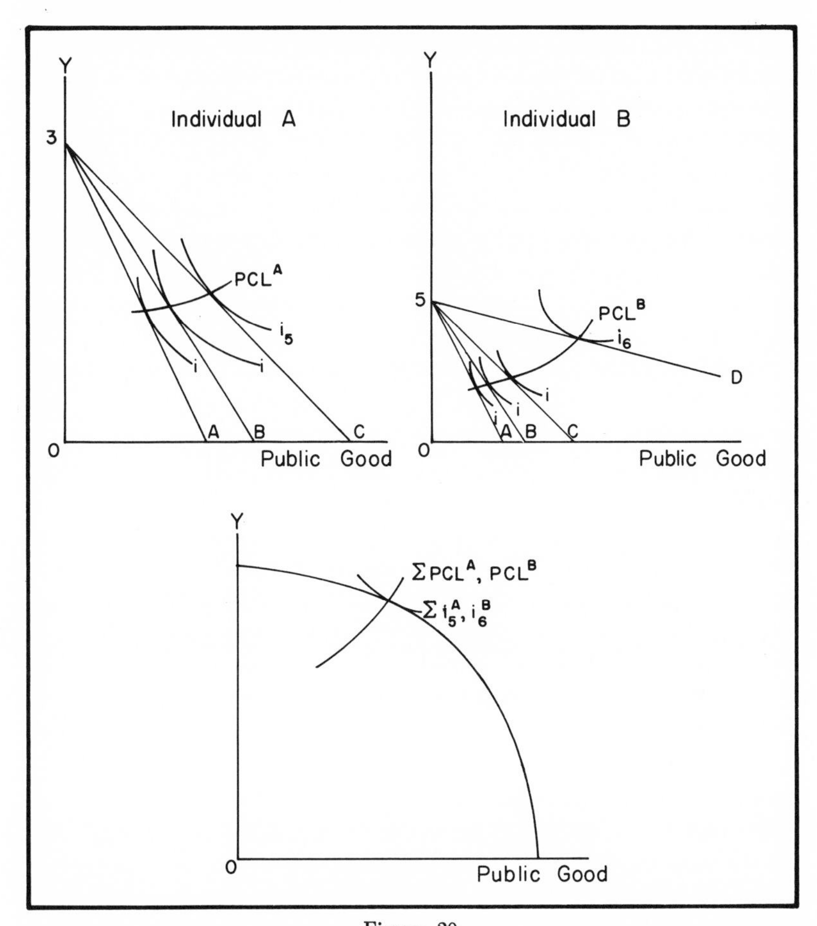

Figure 20.

tions which are necessary for a demand analysis are that individuals do in some way express their demand for the public good as well as the private good and that the government collects the taxes based upon the expressed demand.

Figure 20 is the diagrammatic presentation of the determination of the Pareto optimum allocation of resources with one good defined as a public good. The methodology used is basically the same as in Figure 18 when both goods were private goods sold in the market. The procedure for the development of the individual price consumption lines is not changed by the fact that one of the goods is a public good. However, because of the change in the definition of one of the goods, the procedure for summing the price consumption curves must be changed. The combination of the two goods desired by individual A, when he must take a given quantity of the public good, is added to the combination of the two goods desired by individual B, when he must take the same given quantity of the public good. This change in procedure is just the change to a vertical summation of demand curves from the horizontal summation normally used in the private goods model.[10] The quantity of the public good is held constant and the demand for the two goods is summed, whereas before, the price of X was held constant and the demand for the two goods was summed.

The intersection of the line of the sum of the price consumption lines with the transformation curve provides the Pareto equilibrium so long as the curve of the summation of indifference curves is tangent to the transformation curve.[11] The same basic conditions for general equilibrium and for the Pareto optimum allocation of resources have been met with a public good in the model as with just private goods. The market conditions cannot be assumed to force the allocation of resources toward the optimum since one good is a public good, but this does not mean that such a single optimum does not exist. The government would have to indulge in price discrimination in the sense that the two individuals would not pay the same price for the public good. Individual A will pay for the public good in accordance with the price ratio given by the 3C line of attainable combinations, and individual B will pay for the public good in accordance with the price ratio given by the 5D line of attainable combinations. This, of course, is simply taxation based upon the benefit theory of taxation, where the individual determines the benefit provided by the public good.

10. The vertical summation of demand curves when a public good has the characteristic of joint consumption was developed by Bowen, "Interpretation of Voting in the Allocation of Economic Resources."

11. The method of summing indifference curves is the same as that used by Samuelson. The difference between the methodology used here and Samuelson's is that the modified model employs the price consumption lines of individuals to determine the indifference curves which are to be summed rather than using the arbitrary placement of a combination of the two goods on one individual and permitting the other individual to maximize his satisfaction. The modified model follows market analysis, the Samuelson follows barter exchange analysis.

Comparison of the Equilibriums

Despite the similarity of the analyses and the fact that a single optimum exists in each analysis, the optimum allocation of Figure 18 is different from the optimum allocation of Figure 20. The difference

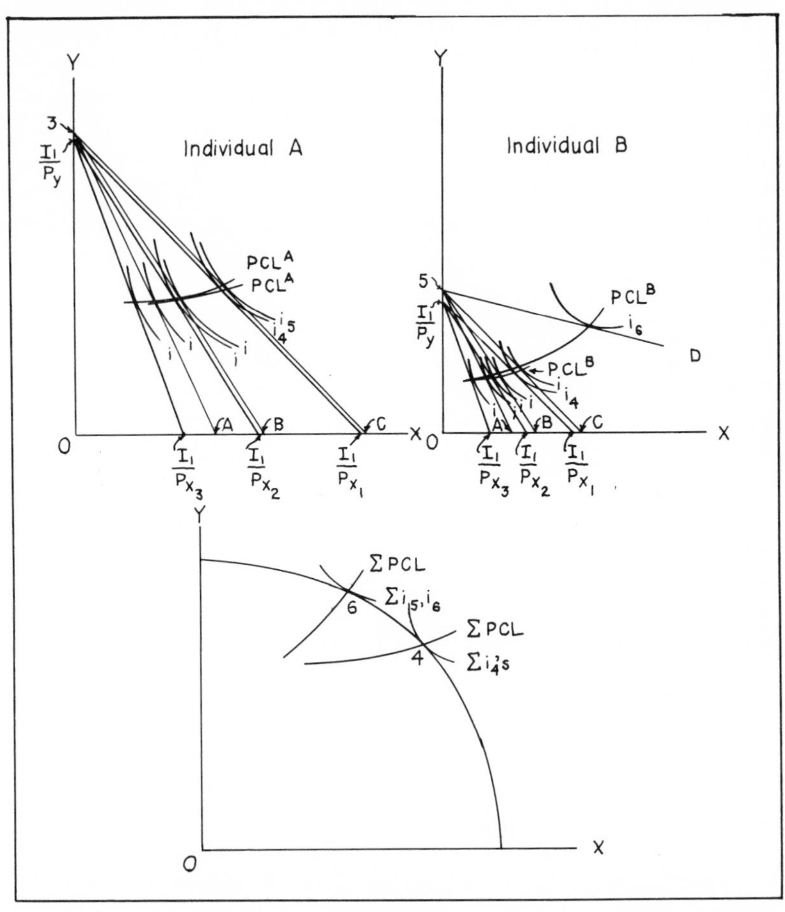

Figure 21.

is shown in Figure 21. It is caused by the fact that the summation of income consumption lines must also be modified when a public good exists in the model. The price demand for the two goods is based upon the vertical summation of demand curves. Therefore, the income demand for the two goods must also be based upon a vertical summation of the individual income consumption lines. The difference in production does also cause a difference in income distribution, but there is still only one distribution of income which is consistent with the assumptions of the model. The difference in production and distribution of income is the logical result of the one good in the second model having the characteristic of joint consumption.

If the private good X in Figure 18 was private protection, the logic of the difference in production may be put in words. For protection to have the characteristics of a private good, it must be assumed that the resources used to protect individual A cannot be used to protect individual B. Thus, individual A hires protection but will not permit the protection to be used to protect individual B. Individual B does the same thing with the protection he purchases. The result is that both individuals (A and B) can purchase their protection at the same price and each will only purchase the quantity he wants at that price. The public good in Figure 20 can also be considered as protection. The difference in the analysis results from the fact that individual A is willing to permit the use of the same resources for the protection of individual B. Likewise, individual B is willing to permit the use of the same resources for the protection of individual A. The result is that the good protection takes on the characteristics of a public good with joint consumption.

Less units of protection can be produced in the second case because the same units are provided to both individuals. If less units are produced, less resources will be used in the good's production. If less resources are used, less total expenditures will be made to whoever is producing the good. Thus more income is available for the purchase of the private good, and more total expenditures will be made to the firms that produce the private good. Both individuals may pay less for the public good protection than they would for the same quantity of the private good protection. The individual who owns the resource which is relatively more productive in the production of protection will lose income relative to the individual who owns the resource which is relatively more productive in the production of the other good. In either case the distribution of income is determined by the original ownership of the resources and by the productivity of the resources used to produce the goods which are demanded. It is simply that less units of protection will be demanded if it is publicly supplied because the same units can be consumed by both individuals.[12] The individuals

12. The individual's demand is not affected by the way in which the good is supplied but the total demand or market demand is affected.

are motivated to express their demand for the public good because, even though they may be discriminated against by having to pay a higher price for the same protection provided to some other individual, the price they pay may be less than they would have to pay if they purchased the same good as a private good. However, the problem still exists that once it is determined that protection is to be supplied publicly, each individual may benefit by not expressing his true demand for protection. The danger is that if everybody tries to conceal his demand, the good will not be supplied publicly, and then all individuals end up paying more for the good than they would have if they had revealed their true demand for the good as a public good.

This explanation of the difference between protection as a public good and as a private good also gives a basis to the paradox that, when asked, people want the government to provide more and more services but want to pay less and less taxes. Such a position is encouraged by the separation of the decision-making process into two parts. This consideration, however, borders on the topic of the next chapter: the criticisms of the application of the theory to the political process.

5. TAXES AND THE POLITICAL PROCESS

There are two broad categories of practical criticism involving taxes and the political process. They are practical criticisms because they do not question the logic of the theory itself, but rather question its application to the real world. The first criticism is that taxes are compulsory payments and cannot be considered analogous to prices in the market. The second criticism is that the political organization of society acts in a unique way and cannot be considered analogous to the market mechanism. Both of these criticisms are implicit in E. R. A. Seligman's history of taxation.[1] He presents the history of taxation as an evolutionary process, moving from the voluntary contributions to tribal chiefs to compulsory payments (such as direct taxation by a central government).[2]

It cannot be denied that the history of taxation does indicate that there have been elements of coercion in taxation in the real world. This is as true about the payments to tribal chiefs as about direct taxation by a central government. To approach the two criticisms logically, it is necessary to separate them. Taxation only exists when a political organization exists, but the first criticism implies that taxes are compulsory per se, no matter what form of political organization exists. Thus, this chapter will take up this criticism by itself and then include it in the analysis of political organizations. It is also necessary to consider the coerciveness relative to some specifically stated criterion.[3] Therefore, the discussion places taxes in a specified political mechanism,

1. *Essays in Taxation,* pp. 1-6.

2. DeViti DeMarco on the other hand has presented the history of taxation as an evolution in forms of voluntary payments, moving from voluntary contributions of goods and services to tribal chiefs to voluntary contributions of money, such as direct taxation by a central government. The existence of constitutional provisions of all representative governments that no tax be determined or collected unless it is approved by the representatives of the people is cited as evidence that taxes are still voluntary in nature (*First Principles of Public Finance,* p. 120).

3. Patinkin gives a good discussion of voluntary and involuntary employment, pointing out the necessity of having an established criterion upon which to evaluate the degree of voluntariness that exists in a particular situation (*Money, Interest and Prices,* pp. 211-14).

and the conclusions are in terms of the degree of coercion relative to prices determined in a specified market situation.[4]

The second criticism is difficult to evaluate in the form in which it is often stated, because to give a complete evaluation, it would require data from real world situations. However, as it is stated here some evaluation is possible. The approach is to define political organizations in the terminology which is common to the analysis of market structures.[5] The conclusions about coercion are in terms of the degree of coercion in one political situation relative to alternative political situations and relative to stated market situations. The very fact that the political organization can be defined in terms similar to those used for market structures suggests that the criticism is not entirely valid. The analysis would also suggest that in the real world taxes are likely to be coercive but that this is because the political organization is not any more likely to be the ideal than is the market structure.

Prices and Taxes

Location of the point at which there is compulsion to act in a specified way in the case of both prices and taxes is one approach to considering the degree of coercion which exists for taxes relative to prices. It is assumed in the discussion that prices are impersonally determined in a purely competitive market situation, and that taxes are impersonally determined by a vote of all the individuals in the society.

The market determines the individual's per-unit price of a good by the equality of the total demand for the good to the total supply of the good. The total demand for the good is the sum of the individual demands. The individual demands are expressed by the individuals' purchasing the good in the quantity desired at the price at which it is offered for sale. The market supply schedule of the good is the sum of the quantities which will be produced by individual firms at various marginal costs. Each firm must offer the good for sale at the per-unit price determined by the entire market for the good, because if a firm offered it at a higher price, the firm would have no sales, and if a

4. Coercion must be discussed in terms of the degree of coercion because compulsion exists in every form of organization. DeViti DeMarco, p. 50n, states: "Compulsion exists in every legal association of individuals; in business organizations, in partnerships, in the church, and especially in labor unions."

5. Haavelmo's discussion of the need for a comparison between alternative economic models or frameworks under which a society may operate is the basis for the approach used here ("Notion of Involuntary Economic Decisions").

firm offered it at a lower price, the firm would in the long run not be able to cover the costs of production.

The vote determines the individual's tax per unit of the good by the equality of the total demand for the good and the marginal cost of the government's production of the good. The total demand for the good is the sum of the individual demands. The individual demands are expressed by the individuals' voting on the quantity that they would desire at each of the various prices possible. The government is under a policy rule to deliver the quantity of the good to every individual in accordance with their expressed demand at the tax-price determined by the equality of the total demand and the marginal costs of production. In both of the above frameworks of analysis, the good can be assumed to be the same good in order to eliminate problems which are related only to the differences in types of goods generally supplied through the use of prices and those generally supplied through the use of taxes.

Basic to the analysis is the issue of what constitutes a sale in the market. The legal and accounting concept of a sale is accepted in this analysis.[6] A sale takes place at the time at which some legally binding evidence of sale has changed hands between the buyer and seller. This means that the point (time) of sale is dependent upon policy rules of the government as to what is considered as legally binding evidence of a sale. It logically follows that a sale in the market is a compulsory act once it is considered to have taken place and that the price is a compulsory payment once the sale has taken place. The legally binding evidence of sale may be the exchange of money or goods for goods. It may also be the joint signing of a contract which legally binds the buyer to pay a certain sum (the sale price) at a specified time and the seller to physically deliver certain goods at a specified time.[7] Neither money nor goods have to physically change hands for a sale to take place. The sale price stated in the contract reflects the per-unit price to the individual as determined in the market.

The point of sale in the case of a tax comes when the individuals of society cast their votes for the quantity of the good desired at the

6. The concept of the point of sale in accounting has been one of the never-ending problems of the accountant. See Paton and Paton, *Corporation Accounts and Statements*, Chap. 10.

7. The laws and customs of nations regarding when and what constitutes a sale vary as to the degree of compulsion exerted by the government to enforce contracts of sale, but most nations whose economic systems can be classified as a market system make the contract for sale a legally binding transaction.

various possible prices. The government is legally bound by a policy rule to establish the price in accordance with the vote of the individuals and the marginal cost of production. The individual is legally bound to accept the quantity of the good that he voted for at the tax-price set in accordance with the established policy rule. The casting of a vote is fully analogous to the signing of a contract. No money or goods change hands between buyer and seller or between taxpayer and government at the point of sale, but once the point of sale is reached, the price or tax and the quantity to be supplied are determined. Once the sale is consummated, the price and tax are both compulsory under the given policy rules. Before the point of sale is reached, there is no market price and likewise no tax-price.

The conclusion that taxes are no more coercive than prices is dependent upon the type of political mechanism which is assumed to exist. The conclusion clearly may not be valid if the political mechanism does not provide a means by which individuals vote for both quantities and prices of each good. The conclusion also may not be valid if the government is not subject to a policy rule which makes taxes and quantity of the good supplied dependent upon the expressed desires of individuals. However, the conclusion makes it clear that there is nothing inherent in the collection of taxes which is more coercive than the collection of a price. Taxes and prices are merely a means of expressing the payment side of a transaction. If coercion exists in taxation, it is not because a tax was used as a means of payment instead of a price. Coercion in taxation must result from some factor which affects the level of taxes to be collected for a good or the quantity of the good to be supplied at a particular level of taxes.

The Market Mechanism and the Political Mechanism

The degree of coercion which exists in the political mechanism relative to that which exists in the market mechanism may be analyzed by defining different political situations (i.e., constitutional rules) in terms of accepted definitions of market situations.[8] The political situations like the market situations are merely hypothetical. Specific real-world political situations come closer to being described by one of

8. For purposes of analysis, Machlup's terminology is adopted because it is based on the psychological aspects of the market which are more easily compared with the psychological aspects of the political situations and because it considers the market situations separately from the concept of the entry of new firms, pliopoly. See *Economics of Sellers' Competition.*

the hypothetical situations than by any of the others. However, no specific real-world political situation is completely described by any of the hypothetical situations. Therefore, the conclusions only refer to hypothetical situations. However, the conclusions are likely to apply for the real-world situation as long as it can be said that a particular real-world political situation is described most closely by one particular hypothetical situation.

Market polypoly is "a state of mind of sellers who know that they have competition, but, in making up their minds about changing their selling or productive policies do not ponder over what their competitors' reactions might be."[9]

Political polypoly is a state of mind of voters who know that they have competitors in the form of other voters with different desires for the same public good, but in making up their minds about voting for particular selling or productive policies do not ponder over what their voter-competitors' reactions might be.

In market polypoly it is usually considered that many buyers and many sellers of a homogeneous product exist. In political polypoly this condition is not of importance. The buyers and sellers are the same individuals in a very direct sense, and the existence of many is assured. All of the individuals which constitute a governmental unit of society are both the buyers and the sellers. A homogeneous product is also not an issue since all voters vote on the production of each good separately. Even where the economic good is considered to be all governmental services, the homogeneous-product condition is met by the political mechanism. The necessary condition is for the government to act in accordance with the vote of the individuals in regard to the quantity and price of the good to be supplied and in accordance with known policy rules of government. The government is thus considered to be nothing more than an organization for the production of the goods and services desired by the individuals of society.

It would be necessary for the voting to be for various quantities of the good at various possible prices in order to meet the conditions of the voluntary exchange theory. A vote on one quantity of the good at one price is not sufficient for a governmental organization which is to be neutral in its own productive activities. The government must know the various combinations of quantities and prices that individuals desire so that they can be compared with the cost of producing the various

9. Machlup, p. 136.

quantities of the good. The essence of such a political situation is that the voter reveals his true preferences without concern for the preferences which others are revealing. The voter knows that the governmental organization is restricted by constitutional rules that require the production policy of the government to be based on the total revealed preferences and costs of production. He also knows the constitutional rules require the taxation policy of the government to be based on the individual preferences for the quantity of the good to be supplied to the individual.

The situations in the market and political mechanism are basically the same as those used in the analysis of taxes and prices. The conclusion, as would be expected, is the same. Only now it can be said that in the market situation and political situation as defined there is no difference in the degree of coercion which would exist.

Market oligopoly is a state of mind of sellers who know that they have competitors, and in making up their minds about changing their selling or production policies do take into consideration what their competitors' reactions might be.[10]

Political oligopoly is a state of mind of governmental officials who know that they have competitors (other governmental officials), and in making up their minds about changing their selling or production policies do take into consideration what the competitors' reactions might be.

The usual cause of market oligopoly is fewness of sellers, which gives the individual seller an awareness of the fact that his actions affect the total market situation and that others notice his actions and react to them. Political oligopoly is similar in that its cause is fewness of voters directly affecting the total market situation. Based on the considerations made in Chapter 3, it is assumed that true preferences would be revealed by individuals if they had the opportunity to vote. Therefore, the difference between political polypoly and political oligopoly is not considered to lie in the desire of the individual to reveal his true preferences. The difference is that in political polypoly the government as an organization is neutral in the determination of quantity of goods to be produced, whereas in political oligopoly the government as an organization is not neutral. The situation is one where the government's selling and production policies are directly determined by a vote of representatives of individuals in the society rather than by a vote of all individuals in the society. Each representa-

10. Machlup, pp. 349-53.

tive is aware of the fact that his actions affect the total market situation and that his competitors notice his actions and react to them. His competitors are the representatives of other individuals in the society. Each representative will temper his actions because of the reactions which might be forthcoming from his competitors. The consequences of the constitutional rules are that the representative is aware of his position in the determination of what and how much at what price is to be produced by the government, and each representative takes into consideration the reactions of other representatives when deciding the preferences he will reveal.

It is still possible, but not necessary, to assume that each representative is attempting to obtain for those whom he represents the quantity and price relationship for each public good which they would desire. If the representative is not attempting to obtain the quantity and price relationship desired by the individuals he represents, it can be considered that coercion is greater than in political polypoly. The higher degree of coercion is a result of a situation where the constitutional rules for the political organization do not permit the type of voting necessary for the government to be neutral in the determination of selling and production policy.

Market monopoly is a state of mind "of a seller who knows neither any individuals nor any particular groups of sellers with whom he is in competition."[11]

Political monopoly is a state of mind of a government official who knows neither any governmental officials nor any particular groups of society (political party) with whom he is in competition.

In market monopoly the individual seller is unaware of a need for considering the reactions of any other sellers in the market. Therefore, his selling and production policies can vary greatly depending upon the motivation which is assumed to be the basis of his actions. He does not believe that the market process will require him to choose any particular policy. The pessimistic monopolist will attempt to make the most of the situation for himself in the short run. The optimistic monopolist may attempt to maintain his position by operating to make the most of the situation in the long run, or he may attempt to maintain his position by advertising and research.[12]

Political monopoly is very similar to market monopoly. The single government official determines the selling and production policies for

11. Machlup, p. 544.
12. Machlup, pp. 555-57.

all public goods without having to compete (vote) with any other governmental officials or political parties. He does not feel a need for considering the reactions of any other representatives of individuals of society because he believes he is the sole representative of the people. However, he may be pessimistic about his position because other representatives of the people may gain popular or military support. Therefore, he will attempt to make the most of the situation for himself in the short run. The political monopolist may also be optimistic about his position because he feels that he can act to prevent any other representative of the people from interfering with his position. As a result, he may operate to make the most of his situation in the long run by relying upon his influence over all possible competitors (all other political officials or all other political parties), or he may attempt to maintain his position by propaganda and by public demonstrations of being the "true" representative of the people.

In political monopoly the taxpayer is reduced to a buyer and serves little, if any, role in the determination of what is to be produced. The potential buyer of a good in the market may be faced, because of the existence of a monopoly seller, with a higher price and therefore must modify the quantity which he purchases. The taxpayer-buyer of a public good has no such opportunity in the case of political monopoly. Public goods which have the characteristics of jointness of supply would have both price and quantity determined independent of the desires of the individual. Even without the characteristic of jointness of supply, in the case of political monopoly, the price and quantity might both be determined arbitrarily. The only opportunities for the individual to obtain his desires in regard to public goods are to escape from the political control of the governmental unit under which he lives or to find some governmental official or group which can take over as the accepted representative of the people.

Coercion in political monopoly is considerably greater than under market monopoly. Market monopoly may cause higher prices than under alternative market situations, but the individual can still adjust the quantity of the good he purchases in accordance with the higher price. Therefore, economic freedom, in one sense at least, is not restricted by the existence of market monopoly. This, however, is not true for political monopoly, where both quantity and price are arbitrarily set by the government. Economic freedom is restricted and coercion does exist. However, the individual can still maximize his satisfaction for all goods, if he considers all governmental services as a single good. In this case, he must alter his consumption of private goods in accordance with the marginal utility per dollar's worth of public goods arbitrarily established by the actions of the political monopolist.

Coercion does not depend upon whether or not the individual can maximize his satisfaction, because the individual can always maximize his satisfaction by altering what he considers as an economic good. The degree of coercion does depend upon the constitutional rules that have been established in the society. A change in the type of the market situation may not affect the degree of coercion that exists. Therefore, the political mechanism is more coercive in nature than the market mechanism unless it is assumed that the political mechanism can be classified as political polypoly.

Pliopoly is the term applied by Machlup to the concept of the entry of new firms in an industry, and it is the existence of pliopoly which tends to eliminate profits in the supply of goods in the market mechanism.[13] Pliopoly, however, does not have to be restricted to the actual entry of new firms. It depends upon an objective evaluation of an outsider as to whether or not it is probable that new firms will enter any given industry.

A similar concept could be developed for the political mechanism.[14] Political pliopoly would refer to the probability that the officials in the government will act in accordance with the desires of the individual in the society. The existence of political pliopoly would, therefore, tend to eliminate coercion in the political mechanism. The objective factors which should be considered in evaluating whether or not governmental officials are likely to so act are complex, but at least a few could be briefly pointed out. The most obvious is whether or not there is a

13. Machlup, p. 211.

14. The political mechanism has no automatic factors which tend to eliminate profits. Whether or not the government should make profits could be established in the form of a constitutional rule, or, as is more likely, in the form of a policy rule of government. The absence or presence of profits in the supply of public goods is of extreme importance, since it determines whether the total budget of the government will be a surplus budget, balanced budget, or deficit budget. Therefore, four possible policy rules are listed with their effects upon the total budget, assuming that they are consistently applied to the pricing of every public good: (1) Average Cost Pricing Rule—balanced budget; (2) Marginal Cost Pricing Rule—budget determined by the value of goods supplied having increasing or decreasing costs; (3) Maximum Production of Public Goods Pricing Rule (i.e., increasing-cost goods at average cost and decreasing-cost goods at marginal cost)—deficit budget; and (4) Minimum Production of Public Goods Pricing Rule (i.e., increasing-cost goods at marginal cost and decreasing-cost goods at average cost)—surplus budget.

regular process by which the individual can express his desires. Another would be whether or not desires are expressed for just a quantity at a given price, or a price at a given quantity, or for various quantities at various possible prices. Still another would be whether or not the governmental policy rules encourage the governmental officials to act in accordance with the desires of the individuals in the society.

It can be considered, from these few factors affecting the existence or nonexistence of political pliopoly, that it would be most likely to occur under the constitutional rules (political situation) classified as political polypoly. The individual voter does have the opportunity to express his desires for the various quantities at the various prices through the voting process, and the policy rules of government require the governmental official to act in accordance with the vote-expressed desires of the individuals in society. However, political pliopoly is not necessary, because governmental officials once in office may be able to circumvent the policy rules or even the constitutional rules. Therefore, political pliopoly is not assured as a component part of political polypoly, but it is most likely to exist under the constitutional rules of that political situation.

In the case of political oligopoly the three objective factors leading to political pliopoly, listed above, are not an inherent part of the political situation. However, this does not rule out the possibility of political pliopoly existing. Under political oligopoly the extent to which the representative can reveal desires different from the "true" desires of the individuals whom he represents depends upon the constitutional rules as to the voting for representatives and upon the constitutional rules[15] as to the voting (balloting) process for specific goods and services. In other words, the likelihood of coercion (the absence of political pliopoly) depends upon whether or not the representative is aware of possible reactions on the part of the voters who choose the representative, and this may in turn depend, at least in part, on the knowledge that the voter is likely to have concerning whether or not

15. DeViti DeMarco states the necessary conditions as follows: "Only if the taxpayers participate in the initial calculation of wants, in which each person judges the economic advisability of paying a given tax in order to obtain in exchange a given public service, and only if this calculation is subjected to annual revision and is open to criticism and continuous public discussion by the Press, the political parties, the parliament, is it possible to have a guarantee that what is involved is a productive public expenditure—that is, one which is regarded as such by those who bear the cost" (*First Principles in Public Finance,* p. 118).

the representative actually does attempt to express the desires of those whom he represents. If the representatives had to cast ballots for various quantities at various prices for each public good because of a constitutional rule, the voters could be aware of the fact that the representative is modifying the individual voters' true preferences. If the representative merely casts a vote for or against a specific quantity and price of each public good, as is usually the case, the voter has less opportunity to be aware of the modification of the individual voters' true preferences. The latter constitutional rule makes it possible for the representative to bargain in the political process, before the decision to produce any public good comes to a ballot, and to assure himself that his vote can be cast without causing reactions on the part of those who vote the representative into office.

Political pliopoly is least likely to occur under the constitutional rules of political monopoly. The only apparent reason that political pliopoly might exist would be the altruistic motives of the governmental official. The existence of policy rules of government, which correspond to the objective factors considered above, would constitute an objective factor indicating the existence of political pliopoly even in the case of political monopoly. The policy rules of the government replace the constitutional rules as objective factors, but policy rules are not controlled or limited by other constitutional rules in the case of political monopoly and therefore depend upon the public spirit of the governmental officials.

The conclusion to be drawn from the analysis of the market mechanism and political mechanism in regard to coercion is that the political mechanism is likely to be more coercive than the market mechanism, but that the degree of coercion in the political mechanism is dependent upon the constitutional rules that establish the particular mechanism. Also it can be concluded that certain constitutional rules and/or policy rules of the government can be considered as objective evidence that the degree of coercion present in any specific political situation is less than it otherwise would have been.

6. APPLICATIONS OF THE SUGGESTED APPROACHES

The approach adopted in Chapter 5 to analyze the criticisms of the operation of the political organization with respect to the price theory of public finance represents a suggested approach to the general area of the effects of political organization on the supply of public goods. This chapter will carry the approach one step further to indicate how it may be applied to the existing area of intergovernmental relations. The second part of this chapter will carry the theoretical framework suggested in Chapter 4 one step further to indicate how it may be applied to the existing area of national goals.

INTERGOVERNMENTAL RELATIONS

Intergovernmental relations has been an area of study within the fields of political science and public finance. In many cases the political scientist does his research in terms of the administrative relations and the economist does his research in terms of the financial relations. The study of administrative relations being independent of the study of financial relations, and vice versa, may lead to conflict between the conclusions derived. Interdisciplinary studies are sometimes used as a method of eliminating the conflict in conclusions, but the results have not been too encouraging. The problem to a large extent lies in the difference of terminology in the two fields, and in the fact that neither the political scientist nor the economist can visualize the importance of small distinctions being made with the special terminology of one field on analysis being employed by the specialist of the other field. There is simply a growing need for specialists trained in more than one field. The economist in the area of intergovernmental relations must understand the terminology and concepts of the political scientist. Furthermore, the economist must recognize how the concepts of political science may modify the economic analysis which is appropriate in a given situation, and how to express the concepts of political science in terms which are consistent with economic terms and frameworks of analysis used in specific situations.

Defining political organizations in terms of economic market structures represents a possible approach to part of the problem. The broad categories of political structures used in Chapter 5 are not adequate.

Market oligopoly is the general case in the real world, just as political oligopoly is the general case for all levels of government in the United States. Oligopoly theory, however, suggests that market oligopoly tends to be unstable and leads to forms of collusion. Therefore, market oligopoly is defined in terms of various forms of collusion. The envisioned area within intergovernmental relations may be termed comparative governmental institutions and would logically follow the same form of definitions as has been adopted in market oligopoly analysis. Each real-world situation would have to be defined in terms of the type of collusion existing in the political organization and the likelihood of pliopoly factors affecting the actions of the political organization.

Examples of the application of this approach are beyond the intended purpose of this monograph. However, the next chapter will in general terms consider the probability of the future use of this and other frameworks derived from the price theory of public finance in empirical or applied areas of studies within the field of economics and political science. It is sufficient here to note the possible application.

National Goals

Contemporary public finance has emphasized the role of government in achieving the goals of the nation. In the United States these goals have been stated by Congress to be related to full employment, price stability, and economic growth. A fourth goal which is important to many nations is related to economic development. The Western nations have not stressed economic development, in part because they consider that they have already achieved a relatively high level of it.

The existing terminology in the literature causes some difficulties because it is often difficult to ascertain the difference, if any, between economic growth and economic development. Changes in Gross National Product or per-capita Gross National Product from one period of time to the next period of time are often thought to measure changes in economic development and economic growth. However, there also exists literature which cites various factors that determine a nation's development and another set of factors that determine a nation's growth. The set of factors cited for each, development and growth, is not entirely consistent between authors, but generally the factors cited as determining economic development have to do with the allocation of given resources with a given level of technology in a period of time, while those determining economic growth have to do with changes in resources and technology over time.

If the above general differences between development and growth are accepted, the suggested approach to the price theory of public finance provides a means of more explicitly stating the differences. Economic development could be expressed in terms of the degree to which the nation has achieved its optimum allocation of resources during a given period of time. Figure 22 illustrates this concept of development. Point A represents the actual allocation between public and private goods, while point B represents the allocation which would result from an optimum allocation of resources. The level of economic development achieved would be expressed in terms of the percentage

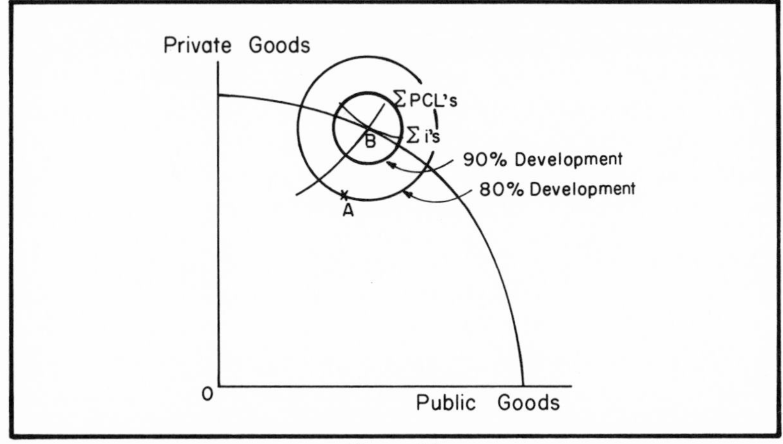

Figure 22.

of full development. The factors determining the level of development achieved would be the structure of the market sector of the economy, the structure of the political sector of the economy, the extent of knowledge about both public and private goods, the measurability of public good demand, the mobility of resources, etc.

Economic growth can be differentiated from economic development with the suggested approach because economic growth takes place over time. Two different concepts of growth are clearly possible with the suggested approach. One concept illustrated in Figure 23 would be that economic growth can be expressed in terms of the change in the optimum allocation of resources (i.e., the change from point B for time period 1 to point C for time period 2). In this context the factors determining economic growth would be changes in the quantity or quality of existing resources, changes in technology, changes in the tastes and preferences of the individuals of the nation, changes in the ownership of economic resources, etc. A second concept of economic growth illustrated in Figure 23 would be that economic growth can be expressed in terms of the change in the transformation curve. In this context the factors determining economic growth would be limited to changes in the quantity and quality of resources and changes in technology. The former concept of economic growth has the advantage of tying growth to the welfare economics concept of the optimum allocation of resources. The latter concept has the advantage of being closer to the literature on the factors determining economic growth.

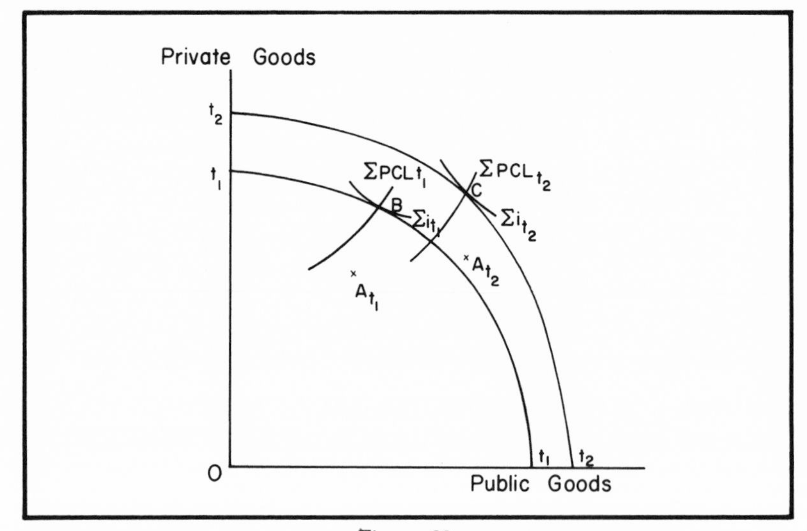

Figure 23.

With either concept of economic growth it is apparent that growth may affect the nation's economic development in subsequent periods of time. This would be particularly true for the first concept, but to some extent true for the second. Economic development in a given period is also likely to affect growth over time. The analysis of these effects is beyond the scope of this monograph. However, it should be noted that Gross National Product, or even per-capita Gross National Product, is not an adequate measure of either economic development or economic growth as they are stated here. Development compares the actual output with a potential output, while growth compares the potential of one period to the potential of another period of time. A change in the actual output from one period to another period of time may be caused by changes in the determinants of development or by growth, with the determinants of development given.

The suggested approach to the price theory of public finance also provides a means of linking the goal of full employment to economic development, economic growth, and the optimum allocation of resources. Full employment exists with any combination of private and public goods which lies on the transformation curve. Thus the goal of full employment is achieved when the actual output for a period is any one of the potential outputs expressed by the transformation curve. Full employment in both of two periods where economic growth has taken place would indicate that the growth has been accompanied

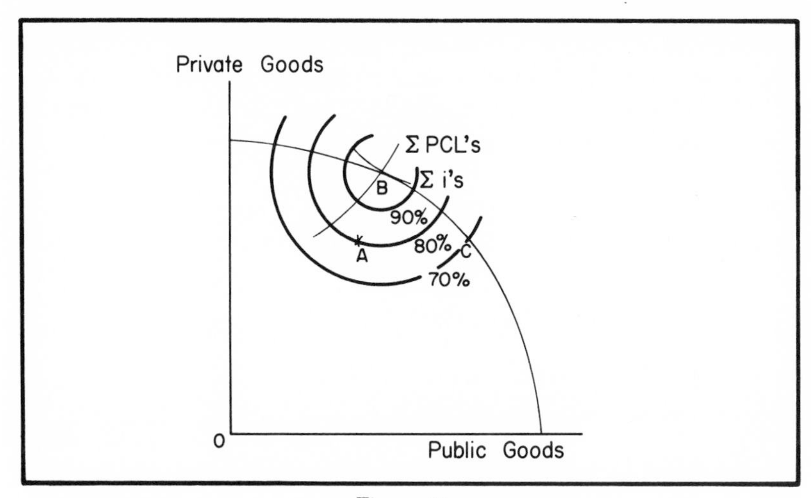

Figure 24.

by an increase in output. However, the achievement of full employment may be in conflict with the achievement of economic development. The possible conflict is expressed by Figure 24.

Point A represents the combination of private and public goods which would actually be produced if the government did not take fiscal policy measures designed to achieve full employment. Point B represents the combination of private and public goods associated with the optimum allocation of resources. Point C represents the actual output that would occur if the government takes certain actions in order to achieve full employment. In the particular case cited the combination given by point A with less than full employment represents a higher level of development than the combination at point

C with full employment. In this case full employment would be achieved by producing more of public goods than the society desired and therefore is in conflict with the goal of economic development. The relative effects of combinations A and C on economic growth, however, may be a different matter. Combination C with full employment may result in more or less economic growth than combination A. Again this is a question which is beyond the bounds of this monograph. The potential of further work within this framework appears to be very great. The interrelationships that exist between full employment, development, and growth cannot be completely specified by the graphs, but the separation of concepts that can be set forth should facilitate further study. One aspect of special note is the effect of changing ownership of resources. The "best" distribution of income is put into the context of happening *over* time rather than happening *in* a period of time. The discussion of the "best" distribution of income without specifying the ownership of resources has been one of the principal problems in welfare economics. In the framework of the suggested approach the problem is put into a more dynamic context which recognizes that the distribution of income (best or otherwise) is the result of organizational structures as well as of the ownership of resources at any given period of time, and that even the ownership of resources over time is the result of the actual distribution of income in past periods of time.

Although the suggested approach to public finance does not provide a diagrammatic framework which simplifies the considerations necessary for the problem of price stability, it may put that problem into a new context which has special merits. In the framework the prices of products may vary as long as the variation does not affect the distribution of expenditures on products and as long as the price paid to the owners of resources varies in accordance with the prices of products without affecting the distribution of income. The level of money income and price levels are related but do not affect the real income and the real level of prices. The problem of price stability may be an important factor in the determination of development and growth but only because price stability may affect market and political structures, market knowledge, technology, tastes and preferences, etc.

The problem of price stability as it is usually stated also involves the redistribution of income from those who are on fixed incomes to those whose income varies with economic conditions. The model of the suggested approach eliminates this aspect of the problem of price stability by the assumptions that all income is spent and that all income is derived from the use of productive resources in the production process. In the real world, money and the process of the creation of money are a source of money income to individuals. The result is that money income is redistributed from what it would be if money were neutral, as it is in the model. Thus, the existence of financial assets in a society is another reason why the optimum allocation of resources (100 per cent development) will not be achieved. As individuals save by making financial investments (purchase financial assets), the money income earned by the owners of the factors of production is transferred into the hands of those who previously owned or created the financial assets. The new owners of the money income are the individuals who then demand products and determine the combination of private and public goods which should be produced. This distribution of income, like a distribution of income resulting from monopsony resource markets, would also affect the achievement of economic development and may have implications for economic growth.

One approach which would bring money as a non-neutral factor into the model would be to accept money as a productive resource. In the real world, money is a necessary factor for the production process to operate efficiently, and the creation of money makes possible changes in market structures. However, the development of a transformation curve from isoquant analysis is very questionable if money is considered one of the resources used in the production process. There appears to be no a priori basis for stating the shape of an isoquant with money as one of the resources.

The answer to this problem is not within the scope of this monograph. However, it is apparent that leaving money neutral in the model may not be an adequate simulation of the real world because money, financial assets, and the process of creating money do affect the distribution of income which determines the demand for products. The inadequacies of the model are the same as most price theory models. Monetary effects are difficult to deal with in most resource allocation models.

7. OTHER APPLICATIONS OF THE THEORY

In Chapter 6 an attempt was made to indicate areas of economics wherein we might make valid applications of the specific framework developed earlier in this monograph. The present chapter is also concerned with the application of the theory, but not within the specific framework developed here. First, two applications of the past will be commented upon, and then the prospects for future applications in general will be considered. The first of the past applications, as in the previous chapter, will deal with an area that may be more appropriately considered as political science. This application applies the price theory of public finance only in that it is an analysis of political behavior in terms of the traditional price theory assumption that individuals attempt to maximize their satisfaction. The second application does not involve an application to specific economic problems, but rather represents one of the broadest applications of the terminology of price theory to public finance in general.

Existing Applications

Buchanan and Tullock in *The Calculus of Consent* begin with the premise that political behavior, just as economic behavior, can be analyzed by making the assumption that individuals attempt to maximize their satisfaction. Under this assumption it might follow that political polypoly would be considered the ideal form of governmental organization. This follows from the fact that with such a political structure the political mechanism works as efficiently as the purely competitive market structure, and the individual maximizes his satisfaction by equating the marginal utility per dollar's worth of all goods, including public goods.

Buchanan and Tullock point out that a representative form of government (political oligopoly) is not inconsistent with rational behavior of individuals, because there may be some costs associated with the act of collective decision-making.[1] There may be costs associated with obtaining any specified number of individuals to vote in favor of any particular proposal, and costs associated with the taking of a vote of all individuals on various quantities and various prices for

1. Page 44.

each public good. The costs can be expected to increase more than proportionately as the number of individuals increases. In obtaining a specified number of individuals to vote in favor of a particular proposal, the costs can be expected to increase more than proportionately as the number of individuals necessary to vote in favor of the proposal increases. The unanimity rule would, therefore, have the greatest cost of decision-making associated with it. Buchanan and Tullock concluded that it can be considered rational for an individual, attempting to maximize his satisfaction, to prefer the representative form of government over one which requires many individuals to vote on the supply of each good produced by the government.[2]

This conclusion is even more likely to hold true if there are additional constitutional rules establishing a system of checks and balances which limit the functions of the various branches of government, so that the branches of government are somewhat analogous to the market organization.[3] The function of the legislative branch can be limited to the interpretation of the quantity and price of particular goods desired by individuals of the society. The function of the executive branch can be limited to the determination of how to combine resources in the production of the goods determined as desirable by the legislative branch. The function of the judicial branch can be limited to the evaluation of whether or not the other two branches of government have acted within all of the constitutional rules established by the society.

However, once established, with the legislative branch interpreting the desires of all individuals of the society, the representatives that make up the legislative branch may come under the pressures of minority groups of individuals organized to obtain exclusive benefits for the group which are to be paid for by all of the individuals of the society.[4] These pressure groups are a natural outgrowth of the system, if the assumptions about rational economic behavior are accepted, because small groups of individuals find that they can gain

2. Pages 115-16.

3. These rules may be considered as additional factors to be considered as evidence that political pliopoly can exist.

4. DeViti DeMarco's conclusions about pressure groups are similar but are stated in terms of his own framework of analysis. The pressure groups are considered to be evidence of a monopolistic element in government. He concluded that if capital-owning pressure groups win, higher prices must be paid to private firms, and if labor pressure groups win, higher prices will have to be paid in the form of higher costs of production (*First Principles of Public Finance*, p. 50).

more in benefits than it costs them to organize and obtain the benefits.[5] The result is that the constitutional rules establishing the representative form of government do not operate as they were intended to operate. The benefits from the goods supplied by the government become separated from the costs (taxes). The majority of the society, rather than the minority of the society, must adjust their private consumption to maximize their satisfaction as a result of the government supply of goods.

Buchanan and Tullock suggest the adoption of a policy rule which would require all goods that benefit a particular minority group be paid for by special taxation of another equal in size minority group. The logic of this rule is that in this manner countervailing powers would be established without causing a further growth of either power.[6]

Buchanan and Tullock also consider the possibility that no matter which of the possible constitutional and policy rules exist, coercion may not exist as long as unanimity exists concerning the rules.[7] In other words, as long as each individual in the society agrees that the rules should exist, it can be assumed that they believe that the gains to be derived from changing to any alternative set of rules do not equal the costs of making the change.[8] However, a point not considered is that some of the costs of changing to an alternative set of constitutional rules may be the direct result of the existing constitutional rules regarding the process necessary in order to obtain a change. This last point may be a basis for the changes in the interpretation of the Constitution in the United States during recent years. The process of changing the Constitution is difficult and involves costs which can be avoided by simply having the Supreme Court reinterpret the existing Constitution in such a way as to accomplish the changes that the individuals of society would write into the Constitution if the costs of doing so were not so great.

In any case the work of Buchanan and Tullock is an interesting application of one of the basic assumptions of price theory to the area of political behavior. It puts political behavior into a frame of reference that the economist should be able to understand more clearly and should be more willing to accept. It also provides a mixing of terminology from the two fields which should lead to a better understanding of concepts in both fields of study.

5. Buchanan and Tullock, pp. 286-87.
6. Pages 291-94.
7. Pages 250-53.
8. Pages 260-62.

Antonio DeViti DeMarco in *First Principles of Public Finance* provides an example of the application of the terminology of price theory to the field of public economics. He does not develop a specific model but merely applies the models and concepts of price theory to his explanation of public finance concepts and to the history of public finance. Therefore, his application primarily deals with the tax side, but he does carefully state that public finance is not just the study of taxation, politics, or law. "The discipline which gives the really necessary and fundamental explanation of the phenomena of public finance is, however, economics."[9] DeViti DeMarco's definition of public finance or public economics gives a still better indication of the extent to which he would apply price or value theory to the public sector of the economy. Public economics "investigates the conditions to which the productive activity of the State must be subjected in order that the *choice of the public services which are produced, the determination of their respective amounts, the distribution of the costs among the consumers, etc.*, may take place according to the principles of theory of value—that is, with the least possible waste of private wealth, in order to attain the greatest satisfaction of collective needs."[10]

This definition contains all of the elements of the voluntary exchange or price theory of public finance. All three of the economic problems related to public finance are specifically stated in relation to the principles of the theory of value (price theory). The function and goal of public economics is to investigate the means of attaining the greatest satisfaction of collective needs with the least possible waste of private wealth. The relationship of this function and goal to price theory is obvious. Also, the definition considers the state as a producer of goods and services and the taxpayer as a consumer. The state is a producer of goods and services not just when the goods resemble goods which can be supplied through the market mechanism but whenever the state satisfies collective needs.

Public goods and services are classified as either "Special Public Services" or "General Public Services." A public good is in the former classification if it meets both of the following criteria: (1) the supply of the service must be technically divisible into salable units; (2) the service must be constantly demanded by individuals.[11] Public

9. Page 34.

10. Page 36.

11. DeViti DeMarco believes that some services such as public safety are an example of a service which is not constantly demanded by individuals. The de-

goods and services fall into the second classification if they do not meet both of the foregoing criteria.

Special public services require fee type pricing which makes their supply somewhat analogous to private goods and services. However, since the government can act monopolistically in the supply of public goods and services, a rule of average cost pricing must be adopted by the government. General public services, on the other hand, are more unique in that they are generally supplied by the government and require a tax type of pricing. With general public services, individual consumption is an unknown quantity. However, this does not rule out the use of value theory in answering the economic questions about their supply. Consumption can be assumed to be proportionate to income. It is an assumption, but DeViti DeMarco contends that it has both an empirical and a logical foundation.

Basing it on this assumption, DeViti DeMarco develops a concept of individual net income. The concept is analogous to the value added concept of gross national product in that individual net incomes can be summed to arrive at a measure of national income. No income is to be counted twice, and no income is to be deducted which is not counted as income of some other individual. Developed in this manner, individual net income is considered an indication of consumption and, therefore, the measure of individual taxable income. If the sum of the individual taxable incomes is greater than national income, double taxation exists. If the sum of the individual taxable income is less than national income, price discrimination exists in the supply of public goods and services.

Price discrimination can exist because of the monopolistic nature of the government in the supply of goods and services. However, DeViti DeMarco also recognizes that the single tax-price is based upon the concepts of pure competition and that care must be used in its application to public goods and services. Multiple pricing does not necessarily mean price discrimination exists, according to DeViti DeMarco. Price discrimination only occurs with general public services when an individual net income is not taxed on a proportionate basis with all other individual net incomes. Multiple pricing, therefore, exists for general public services in that different individuals pay different prices, but price discrimination only occurs when an individual taxable income re-

---

mand only recurs when public safety is actually impaired. Danger is always present but the individual demand for protection is dormant until the danger is recognized by the fact that the service has not been supplied and someone's safety has not been protected.

ceives special treatment.[12] Multiple pricing proportionate to individual taxable income is based on consumption and thereby follows the concepts of value theory. Multiple pricing based on special treatment of particular individual taxable incomes is the result of the monopolistic nature of the government in the supply of goods and services, and is a case of price discrimination. Likewise, in the supply of special public services, multiple pricing may or may not be evidence of price discrimination, depending upon whether or not it is a result of the monopolistic nature of the government in the supply of these goods. When multiple pricing exists because of differential costs, price discrimination does not exist. In fact, in this case a single price would result in price discrimination. However, if multiple pricing exists in the supply of special public services only as a result of the monopolistic nature of the government supply, the multiple pricing does result in price discrimination.

The concept of grouping similar special public services together and using a multiple pricing technique so that the total cost equals total revenue is based upon the monopolistic nature of the supply of public goods, and therefore constitutes a form of price discrimination.[13] Using tax pricing for special public services or attempting to supply general public services by using a fee type pricing system also is based on the monopolistic nature of government, and is a form of price discrimination. Also, the concept of using the total budget of the government, which includes both special and general public services, as a basis for the supply of public goods would result in price discrimination. However, the total budget of just general public services is to be used as a basis for the determination of what to produce, how much to produce, and how much to charge. Here individual consumption is assumed to be proportionate to individual net income, and the sum of all individual net incomes should equal national income.

DeViti DeMarco's work represents an era of Italian economics which saw a fairly wide application of price theory concepts to the field of public finance and to some extent crossing over to the area of political science. The work of Maffeo Pantaleoni is an example of the latter. The era, however, died out, and this type of broad application of price theory concepts and terminology to public finance and the political organization has to some extent died with it. The works of Wicksell, Lindahl, Bowen, Kafoglis, Buchanan, and Tullock are modern examples of appli-

12. Pages 114-15.
13. Pages 81-88.

cation, but none of these carry the application of price theory terminology as far as did DeViti DeMarco.

Future Application

The applicability and limitations of the price theory of public finance to three broad areas of study are considered in the remainder of this chapter. The three areas of application are (1) as an explanation of the real world, (2) as a framework for policy proposals, and (3) as a framework for discussing concepts of public finance.

The political mechanism which is necessary for the government to be able to provide an optimum allocation of resources is not likely to exist in the real world. Therefore, political polypoly is not an explanation of the operation of the political process in the real world. Neither is the optimum allocation of resources model an explanation of the actual allocation of resources by the government in the real world. These limitations are obvious to even the casual observer of the actual political process who understands the necessary conditions of political polypoly and of the optimum allocation of resources model. However, this consideration does not have to affect the acceptance of the price theory of public finance as an explanation of real-world events. The same type of observations can be made in relation to the pure competition model and the real-world market situations. Market oligopoly is the most likely market situation in the real world, just as political oligopoly is the most likely political situation. The difference which affects the relative acceptability of the two frameworks of analysis lies in the fact that the economic implications of market oligopoly have been developed and studied by leading economists of England and the United States, while the economic implications of political oligopoly have never been systematically set forth. The development of precise definitions for, and of analysis of the economic implications of, political situations is essential to the future application of the price theory of public finance to real-world situations.

The political polypoly model which does provide an optimum allocation of resources is important to economic analysis, even if it does not provide an explanation of the operation of the real-world political process or of the operation of the real-world allocation of resources to public goods. In a democratic representative society it is likely that the general principles of the optimum allocation of resources model can be applied to specific real-world allocation problems.

In any case, there is no apparent reason why the tools of price theory analysis would not provide insights into the allocation of resources to public goods in the real world. The political situation which exists will have to be taken into consideration, but this limitation is not sufficient reason for rejecting price theory tools of analysis.

The hypothetical political situation defined as political polypoly and the optimum allocation of resources model do provide objective criteria for making policy proposals. However, there are many problems of applying the conditions of the hypothetical situation and of the model to real-world allocation problems. Whether or not these problems of application can be overcome cannot be known until attempts are made to interpret the concepts and arrive at specific proposals. In any case, it is likely that any proposals for sweeping changes in the operation of government would not be accepted in our society. Policy proposals by economists are called for by our society and by the governmental organizations which represent society. Therefore, as particular situations arise, the economist can make proposals which will tend to make the operation of government come closer to political polypoly and the production of public goods come closer to the optimum allocation of resources if the theoretical concepts can be translated into reasonable policy proposals.

Political polypoly as a hypothetical set of constitutional rules is primarily the concern of the political scientist. However, the economist may very well be concerned with proposed changes in constitutional rules which affect the government's ability to interpret the demands of individuals for public goods. One example of such a change can here be considered for illustrative purposes. The state of Oklahoma has considered several proposed changes in its constitution relating to representation in its legislative branch. A non-population basis for representation is likely to result in the favored group having a greater vote in the allocation of resources by the state. The economist has a responsibility to point out what effects the various proposals might have upon the allocation of resources.

The optimum allocation of resources model and policy rules which determine the role of government in the production of public goods are more directly the concern of the economist. This fact does not imply that the economist should propose a policy rule that will make the optimum allocation of resources the role of government in the production of public goods. Such a policy rule would probably not be accepted by our society. Other considerations must be taken into account. These other considerations, however, do not prevent the economist from evaluating specific proposals in particular situations and stating whether or not the proposal will cause the allocation of resources to correspond more closely to the optimum allocation than the present allocation of resources. In other words, the optimum allocation of resources can serve as a standard of reference for policy proposals by economists. In many specific allocation problems it may be that the proposal based upon the optimum allocation of resources would be acceptable to our society. The problems of measurement and interpretation of the situation in this case would be the primary stumbling blocks to the acceptance of the proposals. In any case, the price theory of public finance provides the theoretical framework for objectively analyzing policy proposals. Whether or not the proposals would be accepted by our society with our existing political situation can only be answered when specific proposals are actually made.

The area of most importance to the present application of the price theory of public finance is the discussion of concepts of public finance. Future applications of the theory to specific allocation problems ultimately depend upon whether or not economists think of public finance in terms of applying price theory concepts to public goods. If economists discuss public finance concepts in terms of price theory concepts, the application of the theory to specific problems will more or less naturally follow.

DeViti DeMarco's work is a classic example of what can be done in this area. The general principles of price theory analysis can be applied to existing concepts in public finance. The basic problem lies in the economists' existing views that the government acts in an arbitrary manner not related to the demands of society for public goods and that taxes are coercive payments. Taxes can be discussed as prices paid for the goods and services produced by the government. The government can be discussed as a producer of economic goods. It may be necessary to recognize the fact that the political process is likely to be more coercive than the market process in the allocation of resources. This limitation need not interfere with discussing the production of public goods in terms of the process being a transaction which has a payment side and a production side that are determined by supply and demand.

Kafoglis' work in defining public goods in terms of the existence of external economies and diseconomies is another example of what can be done to apply price theory concepts to the discussion of concepts of public finance. It is conceivable to define public finance as the study of goods which have the characteristics of external economies or external diseconomies. Any good with these characteristics is of public concern. It therefore may be considered as a public good even if it is not presently produced by the government. In any case, it appears that a great deal more work can be done in the area of defining public goods as to the characteristics of the goods. National defense can be discussed as a good with the characteristic of jointness of consumption. The allocation of resources to national defense can be discussed in terms of the supply and demand for national defense. That the existing political mechanism cannot perfectly measure the demand must enter the discussion, but this need not preclude the discussion of national defense as a public good.

The main point to be made is that the future development and application of the voluntary exchange or price theory of public finance depend to a large extent upon the application of the general principles of price theory analysis to existing concepts of public finance. If and when economists discuss taxes as prices, the government as a producer, the activities of government as public goods, and the allocation of resources by government based upon supply and demand, the price theory of public finance will be applied to specific problems of government.

SELECTED BIBLIOGRAPHY

BOOKS

American Economic Association Committee. *A Survey of Contemporary Economics*. Ed. B. F. Haley. Homewood, Ill.: Richard D. Irwin, 1952.

Arrow, Kenneth J. *Social Choice and Individual Values*. New York: John Wiley and Sons, 1951.

Benson, Charles S. *The Economics of Public Education*. Boston: Houghton Mifflin Co., 1961.

Bentham, Jeremy. *The Theory of Legislation*. Ed. C. K. Ogden. New York: Harcourt, Brace and Co., 1931.

Boulding, Kenneth E. *Principles of Economic Policy*. Englewood Cliffs, N. J.: Prentice-Hall, 1958.

Bowen, Howard R. *Toward Social Economy*. New York: Rinehart and Co., 1948.

Bryce, Murray D. *Industrial Development*. New York: McGraw-Hill Book Co., 1960.

Buchanan, James M. *The Public Finances*. Homewood: Richard D. Irwin, 1960.

———. *Public Principles of Public Debt*. Homewood: Richard D. Irwin, 1958.

Buchanan, James M., and Gordon Tullock. *The Calculus of Consent*. Ann Arbor: University of Michigan Press, 1962.

Colm, Gerhard. *Essays in Public Finance and Fiscal Policy*. New York: Oxford University Press, 1955.

Dahl, Robert A., and Charles E. Lindblom. *Politics, Economics and Welfare*. New York: Harper and Brothers, 1953.

DeViti DeMarco, Antonio. *First Principles of Public Finance*. Trans. Edith Pavlo Marget. London: Jonathan Cape, 1936.

Downs, Anthony. *An Economic Theory of Democracy*. New York: Harper and Brothers, 1957.

Gough, J. W. *The Social Contract*, 2d ed. London: Oxford University Press, 1957.

Hayek, Friedrich A. *Individualism and Economic Order*. Chicago: University of Chicago Press, 1948.

Hicks, Ursula K. *Public Finance*. New York: Pitman Publishing Corp., 1947.

Jevons, William Stanley. *The Theory of Political Economy*, 4th ed. London: Macmillan and Co., 1924.

Kafoglis, Milton Z. *Welfare Economics and Subsidy Programs*. Gainesville: University of Florida Press, 1962.

Knight, Frank H. *Freedom and Reform*. New York: Harper and Brothers, 1947.

Lerner, Abba P. *The Economics of Control*. New York: Macmillan Co., 1944.

Leftwich, Richard H. *The Price System and Resource Allocation*. New York: Holt, Rinehart, and Winston, 1960.

Little, I. M. D. *A Critique of Welfare Economics*. London: Oxford University Press, 1957.

Locke, John. *Locke and Liberty*. Ed. Massimo Salvadori. London: Pall Mall Press, 1960.

———. *The Second Treatise of Government*. Ed. Thomas P. Peardon, New York: Liberal Arts Press, 1952.

Machlup, Fritz. *The Economics of Sellers' Competition*. Baltimore: Johns Hopkins Press, 1952.

Musgrave, Richard A. *The Theory of Public Finance*. New York: McGraw-Hill Book Co., 1959.

Musgrave, Richard A. and Alan T. Peacock (eds.) *Classics in the Theory of Public Finance.* New York: Macmillan Co., 1958.

National Bureau of Economic Research. *Public Finances: Needs, Sources, and Utilization.* Princeton: Princeton University Press, 1961.

Patinkin, Don. *Money, Interest, and Prices.* Evanston, Ill.: Row, Peterson and Co., 1956.

Paton, William, and William Paton, Jr. *Corporation Accounts and Statements.* New York: Macmillan Co., 1955.

Pigou, A. C. *A Study in Public Finance,* 3d ed. London: Macmillan and Co., 1949.

———. *The Economics of Welfare,* 2d ed. London: Macmillan and Co., 1924.

Rolph, Earl R. *The Theory of Fiscal Economics.* Berkeley: University of California Press, 1954.

Samuelson, Paul A. *Foundations of Economic Analysis.* Cambridge: Harvard University Press, 1948.

Seligman, Ben B. *Main Currents in Modern Economics.* Glencoe, Ill.: Free Press, 1962.

Seligman, Edwin R. A. *Essays in Taxation.* London: Macmillan Co., 1913.

———. *Studies in Public Finance.* New York: Macmillan Co., 1925.

Smith, Adam. *An Inquiry into the Nature and Causes of the Wealth of Nations.* Ed. Edwin Cannan. New York: Random House, 1937.

Snider, Delbert A. *Economics: Principles and Issues.* Homewood, Ill.: Dorsey Press, 1962.

Strayer, Paul J. *Fiscal Policy and Politics.* New York: Harper and Brothers, 1958.

Uhr, Carl G. *Economic Doctrines of Knut Wicksell.* Berkeley: University of California Press, 1960.

JOURNALS

Bator, Francis M. "The Simple Analytics of Welfare Maximization," *American Economic Review,* XLVII (March, 1957), 23-24.

Bowen, Howard R. "The Interpretation of Voting in the Allocation of Economic Resources," *Quarterly Journal of Economics,* LVII (November, 1943), 27-49.

Bowen, William G., *et al.* "The Public Debt: A Burden on Future Generations," *American Economic Review,* L (September, 1960).

Brown, Harry G. "The Incidence of a General Output or a General Sales Tax," *Journal of Political Economy,* XLVII (April, 1939), 254.

Buchanan, James M. "Individual Choice in Voting and the Market," *Journal of Political Economy,* LXII (1954), 334-43.

———. "Politics, Policy, and the Pigovian Margins," *Economica,* XXIX, New Series (February, 1962).

———. "Pricing of Highway Services," *National Tax Journal,* V (June, 1952), 97-107.

———. "The Pure Theory of Government Finance: A Suggested Approach," *Journal of Political Economy,* LVII (December, 1949), 496-505.

Colm, Gerhard. "In Defense of the Public Interest," *Social Research,* XXVII (1960), 295-307.

Downs, Anthony. "The Public Interest: Its Meaning in a Democracy," *Social Research,* XXIX (1962), 1.

Due, John F. "Toward a General Theory of Sales Tax Incidence," *Quarterly Journal of Economics,* LXVII (May, 1963).

Graff, J. DeV. "On Making a Recommendation in a Democracy," *Economic Journal,* LXXII (June, 1962), 293.

Haavelmo, Trygve. "The Notion of Involuntary Economic Decisions," *Econometrica*, XVII (1950), 1.

Head, J. G. "Public Goods and Public Policy," *Public Finance*, XVII (1962).

Kafoglis, Milton Z. "Highway Policy and External Economies," *National Tax Journal*, XVI (March, 1963), 68.

———. "Price Theory and Tax Equity in Highway Finance," *Highway Research Board Bulletin 222*. Washington D. C.: National Academy of Sciences, 1959.

Kendrick, M. Slade. "Public Expenditure: A Neglected Consideration in Tax Incidence Theory," *American Economic Review*, XX (March, 1930).

Knight, Frank H. "Some Fallacies in the Interpretation of Social Cost," *Quarterly Journal of Economics*, XXXVIII (1924), 586-606.

Leibenstein, Harvey. "Notes on Welfare Economics and Theory of Democracy," *Economic Journal*, LXXII (June, 1962), 299.

Meade, James E. "External Economies and Diseconomies in a Competitive Situation," *Economic Journal*, LXI (August, 1952), 54-67.

Musgrave, Richard A. "The Voluntary Exchange Theory of Public Finance," *Quarterly Journal of Economics*, LIII (February, 1939), 212.

Robertson, D. H. "Those Empty Boxes," *Economic Journal*, XXXIV (March, 1924), 16-21.

Samuelson, Paul A. "Aspects of Public Expenditure Theories," *Review of Economics and Statistics*, XL (November, 1958).

———. "Diagrammatic Exposition of a Theory of Public Expenditures," *Review of Economics and Statistics*, XXXVII (November, 1955), pp. 350-56.

———. "The Pure Theory of Public Expenditure," *Review of Economics and Statistics*, XXXVI (November, 1954).

Scitovsky, Tibor. "The State of Welfare Economics," *American Economic Review*, LXI (1951).

———. "Two Types of External Economies," *Journal of Political Economy*, LXII (1954), 143-51.

Sharp, Ansel M. "A General Theory of the Public Debt," *American Journal of Economics and Sociology*, XIX (October, 1959).

———, and Donald R. Escarraz, "A Reconsideration of the Price or Exchange Theory of Public Finance," *Southern Economic Journal* (October, 1964).

Tiebout, Charles M. "A Pure Theory of Local Expenditures," *Journal of Political Economy*, LXIV (October, 1956), 416-24.

Weisbore, Burton A. "Education and Investment in Human Capital," *Journal of Political Economy*, LXX (Supplement, October, 1962), 106-23.

Young, Allyn. "Pigou's Wealth and Welfare," *Quarterly Journal of Economics*, XXVII (August, 1913), 671-86.